SIBERIA

SIBERIA

Madelyn Klein Anderson

Illustrated with photographs

DODD, MEAD & COMPANY
New York

Published by Dodd, Mead & Company, Inc.,
71 Fifth Avenue, New York, N. Y. 10003
Manufactured in the United States of America

Designed by Joy Taylor

1 2 3 4 5 6 7 8 9 10

Library of Congress Cataloging-in-Publication Data

Anderson, Madelyn Klein.
  Siberia.

  Includes index.
  Summary: Examines the history, people, industry,
and agriculture of the mysterious Russian lands
which comprise one-third of the Asian continent.
  1. Siberia (R.S.F.S.R.)—Juvenile literature.
[1. Siberia (R.S.F.S.R.)] I. title.
DK753.A63 1987   957'.0854   87-19922
ISBN 0-396-08662-4

Acknowledgments

For their invaluable contributions, I am grateful to Ann Shaloff for her expert reading of the manuscript; to Nicholas Mango for allowing me access to his expert paper on water supply and hydroelectricity in Siberia; to Dr. Robert A. Karlowich for his expert knowledge of sources; and to my son, Justin Lee Anderson, for his expert—and extensive—backup.

To Marjorie Zaum Goldenthal my special thanks for providing the memory of a Czarist Russian-Jewish lullaby:

> *They writhe and shriek, the black clouds and icy winds*
> *That bring greetings from your father in Siberia, my child.*
> *They writhe and shriek, the black clouds from that icy land*
> *Where your dear father must stay, a spade in his hand.*

The Illustrations

Many of the pictures in this book are old and rare photographs, used in order to preserve these glimpses into living history. The photographs on pages 40 and 115 and the map on page 130 are courtesy of the U.S. Coast Guard. The map of the USSR on pages 4–5 is from PIP, Inc., by Robin Greaves.

Contents

Introduction   3

1. A Siberian Mystery   11

2. The Huns, the Horde, and the Terrible   18

3. The Wild, Wild East   27

4. Expanding Frontiers   36

5. Of Wars and Back Doors   45

6. The Allies and the Revolutionaries   63

7. The Prisoners of Siberia   77

8. The Prisoners of Stalin   98

9. The Great Patriotic War   110

10. Behind the Iron/Ice Curtain   120

Index   143

SIBERIA

Introduction

F EW PLACES in the world seem so mysterious as Siberia. And one of the mysteries of Siberia is: where is it? Defining its boundaries, understanding its identity, is not simple.

We know, of course, that Siberia is in the Soviet Union. The Soviet Union or, officially, the Union of Soviet Socialist Republics, straddles two continents, Europe and Asia. Fifteen Republics make up the Union—the Russian Soviet Federated Socialist Republic and the Soviet Socialist Republics of Belorussia, Ukraine, Georgia, Armenia, Azerbaijan, Latvia, Estonia, Lithuania, Moldavia, and the Central Asian Republics of Kazakhstan, Uzbekistan, Kirgizia, Tadzhikistan, and Turkmenia. You can see that Siberia is not one of the Soviet Union Republics. The Republics are broken up into varying numbers and kinds of administrative units—autonomous republics, autonomous oblasts, oblasts, national okrugs, rayons, krays—but Siberia is none of these, either. Siberia has no administrative identity.

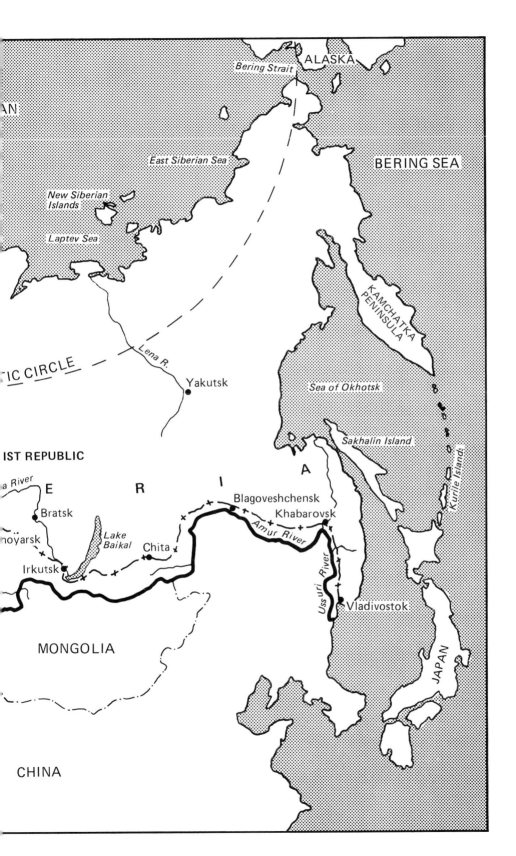

ALASKA

Bering Strait

BERING SEA

East Siberian Sea

New Siberian Islands

Laptev Sea

KAMCHATKA PENINSULA

IC CIRCLE

Lena R.

Yakutsk

Sea of Okhotsk

Sakhalin Island

IST REPUBLIC

a River

E   R   I

Bratsk

Lake Baikal

noyarsk

Chita

Irkutsk

A

Blagoveshchensk

Khabarovsk

Amur River

Ussuri River

Kurile Island

Vladivostok

MONGOLIA

JAPAN

CHINA

Yet it is an area larger in size than the United States and comprises one-third of the Asian continent, and its name is known to all the world—but the origin of that name is another mystery.

There are several interpretations of Siberia's boundaries. One is, very simply, all of the Soviet Union's territory in Asia. This definition includes the Central Asian Republics, and, except for one section of southern Kazakhstan, the Soviets do not consider these states as part of Siberia. Once the fabled land of Turkestan, their history and culture have little to do with Siberia. A more meaningful definition for Siberia is that part of the Russian Soviet Federated Socialist Republic, or the RSFSR, that lies on the Asian continent. The RSFSR, often called simply "Russia," is the largest and most important of the fifteen Republics of the Soviet Union economically and politically. Its capital, Moscow, is also the capital of the entire country. In territory it covers three-quarters of the Soviet Union and stretches over eleven time zones from Europe through Asia to the Pacific Ocean. And within Russia, Siberia reaches from China, Mongolia, and Korea in the south to only some 800 miles from the North Pole.

For one reason or another, possibly because of its reputation, possibly to make it less unwieldy, there seems to be a tendency in the Soviet Union to place more and more limits on Siberia's geography. Some definitions exclude the high Arctic, some the Maritime Kray (Archipelago) and the Pacific islands; some exclude the entire Far Eastern section, calling it instead the Russian or Soviet Far East. Some definitions exclude the eastern Urals, in Asia, because it seems sensible to regard the Urals region as one entity. One can add the western or European Urals for the same reason, but this adds rather than subtracts from Siberia's girth. Shrinking its boundaries makes little difference. Siberia is far more than a place—it is a state of mind.

There is the problem, too, of inner boundaries, which seem to float and change from one information source to another. There is Western Siberia, Central Siberia, and Eastern and Far Eastern Siberia—except that Central may be called Eastern, and Eastern is often combined with Far Eastern. There is no reason to complicate things by attempting to give the many various definitions of these sections. We will use the sections: Western, the Asian side of the Ural Mountains; Central, the area around the Yenisei River; Eastern, the area around Chita; Far Eastern, the Pacific coast area. A general idea and a look at the map should be enough. North-to-south can get complicated also, unless one uses geologic terms: in the south are *steppes* or plains and a belt of rich black earth called *chernozem* (a name adopted by many languages to denote land of great fertility); in what is roughly the middle there are three million square miles of *taiga* or forest; and above that lies the barren tundra of the high Arctic.

A word about names—of people, places, and things. Russians—and the majority of Siberians are Russians—have at least three: a given name, a patronymic, and a surname. The first name and patronymic are a common form of address used. A patronymic is the father's first name plus a masculine or feminine suffix, depending on the bearer's sex. The form of the suffix depends on the name to which it is attached. It is usually but not always "ovich" or "evich" for men and "ovna" or "evna" for women, *i.e.*, Nikolayevich for men, Nikolayevna for women. The great ballerina Pavlova's full name was Anna Pavlovna Pavlova, and she would have been addressed as "Anna Pavlovna," with no preceding honorific. A woman's marriage name takes a feminine ending and so is slightly different from her husband's: Tolstoy's famous Anna Karenina is the wife of Alexei Karenin, his Princess Elizabeth Bolkonskaya in *War and Peace* the wife of Prince Andre Bolkonsky. Since the Revolution of 1917, many wives keep their maiden names. Lenin's wife was Nadezhda Krupskaya. The wife of the famous dissident, Andre Sakharov, is Yelena Bonner. Many revolutionaries changed their names; the reasons were various. Most, were imprisoned at one time or another in Siberia and sought anonymity. Possibly it was to avoid identification as Jews, or to make themselves more memorable. Stalin, from the German word for steel, was born Dzhugashvili; Lenin was Ul'yanov. (The apostrophe softens the preceding consonant.) Not only revolutionaries changed their names. Rasputin, whose evil influence helped bring about the downfall of the Russian monarchy, was born Novykh.

After the Communist Revolution in 1917, place names changed. Names based on royalty or saints were out, Communist names were in. St. Petersburg became Petrograd, and when Lenin died in 1924 the city was renamed Leningrad in his honor. Names of many native tribes were also changed. The Tungus, for instance, became the Evenki, the Chukchi became the Woravetlans, and the Samoyeds broke into three: the Nenets or Nentsy, the Taymyr, and the Yamal. Changes were made to more historically correct names or to eliminate names that were considered somewhat unflattering, just as in America "Inuit" is preferable to "Eskimo," a name derived from the French word for eaters of raw meat, and "Native American" is preferred over "Indian." Name changes among native groups also reflect different systems of classification. They are almost hopelessly complicated, and it is not within the scope of this book to track them.

When Peter the Great modernized Russia he ordered that

the Russian Cyrillic alphabet, based on Greek, be simplified, using Roman letters where possible. The possibilities were not that many, and the Roman letters can confuse. While K, T, and M sound like the English, B sounds like V, C is like S. The Provisional Government that ruled Russia briefly in 1917 further simplified the alphabet and spelling. Most nationalities in the Soviet Union have their own languages that use the Russian alphabet with some variations. But Estonian, Latvian, and Lithuanian languages use the Latin alphabet, and so do the German, Finnish, Polish, and Hungarian.

Translations from Russian to other languages may be phonetic, using symbols and combinations of letters to convey the sound of the word, or transliterations—letter-for-letter translations. And some simplify, for instance, by dropping either i or y when they come together: Dmitriy may become Dmitri or Dmitry. "Y" seems particularly mobile and often appears or disappears. You might find the Siberian city once called Ekaterinburg spelled Yekaterinburg, for instance. There is no universal standard. No attempt was made to stay with one system in this book, but that does not mean that any of the spellings are wrong; they are just variants.

A word about dates. The Russians used the Julian calendar until 1918, when the Bolsheviks changed to the Gregorian calendar used by most of the rest of the world. The Soviets refer to "Old Style" (O.S.) dates and "New Style" (N.S.). Followers of the Russian Orthodox Church around the world use the Old Style for celebrating religious events—Christmas, Easter, and the like. The only confusion for readers may arise from the fact that the Soviet Union celebrates the anniversary of the October Revolution of 1917 on November 7 instead of October 25. The Bolsheviks also changed the names of days of the week to numbers, abolished Sunday as a day off, and used five- and later six-day periods in place of weeks. This was changed back again in 1940, when the Soviet Union was allied with Germany and war conditions mandated the coordination of time frames.

The introduction having been made, the story of Siberia begins—with a big bang . . .

1

A Siberian Mystery

O N A J U N E morning in Central Siberia in the year 1908, a streak of fire brighter than the sun flashes through the sky, leaving in its wake a trail of monstrous thunderclaps. Then all the thunder is gathered up in one final burst, as an explosion shakes the earth and sends a pillar of flame stretching up to the heavens. Huge clouds of black dust darken the sky, and black rain falls.

The column of flame can be seen for hundreds of miles. Waves of heat set off fires in the forest that burn for days. Shock waves shake and shatter windows and doors and roofs. People are tossed about, deafened by the sound and made mute. Miraculously, no one is killed or even seriously hurt—but then there are few people in this forestland in Siberia called the *taiga*. An entire herd of reindeer disappears in the explosion, however. More will die later of a disease unknown to the native herdsmen, a disease that causes scabs to form on their hides.

Many trees of the *taiga* are stripped bare of leaves and branches and bark and stand bare, like telephone poles. Still other trees lie in a circular pattern, fanning out from one central point, as if some giant hand had carefully laid them down. The permafrost, permanently frozen ground, melts from the great heat, and the local streams fill to overflowing.

Observatories as far away as Washington, D.C., register the disturbance as an earthquake, still another in that quake-ridden vastness. Or was it a meteor strike? The Russians are busy with other matters and pay little attention. Many months of difficult travel would be necessary to find the site, and by then what difference would it make?

In Great Britain sudden changes in atmospheric pressure and magnetic power are noted. All of Europe reports magnificent sunsets, sudden dawn at midnight, and abnormal lights and colors in the sky. But no one equates these atmospheric changes with the event in Siberia. Outside of Russia no one knows of it, and in Russia only a few short newspaper articles tell of it.

But the natives of the region, the Tunguses, remember the explosion and the fire. To them, it is still another proof of the powers of evil spirits. They sacrifice reindeer to placate the spirits, and they never again enter the area.

Then, in 1921, the new Communist government sends an expedition from the Academy of Sciences into Siberia to find the site. They are looking for meteorites and are following clues from old reports of possible strikes. This is not out of any desire for scientific knowledge. There is little time for that during those hectic years after the Revolution. What the government is interested in is the wealth of iron, nickel, platinum, and other metals that form the mass of some meteorites. Only the year before, a meteorite containing some

60 tons of valuable iron was found in South Africa, so this is no harebrained scheme. The head of the Academy's expedition, Leonid Kulik, had read the newspaper accounts of the 1908 explosion and had thought at the time that this was a meteorite fall. He was puzzled, however, by the reports of great heat that accompanied the explosion. This is not typical of meteorite falls. Now, thirteen years later, Kulik is eager to find answers. The expedition treks out to the Tungus River area of Siberia and questions witnesses. There is not enough time before the great cold of winter sets in to do more than this, or even to find the exact site.

Over the years, other reports are collected, and the Academy uses them to try to pinpoint the supposed meteor strike. In 1927, Kulik is finally able to bring another expedition into Siberia. The trip through the *taiga* is terrible, every step hazardous. The trees are dense and lean crazily in all directions, their roots barely grasping the ground that the summer thaw has turned into muddy swampland. The men slide and slip and are tripped up by the loose roots and scratched and bruised by the branches. Infection sets into their cuts, scurvy swells their legs and loosens their teeth. Insects, the scourge of summer in the Arctic and subarctic, drive them wild. Finally, their Tungus guides bring them within sight of the explosion area. The guides disappear—they will not go into the home of evil spirits. And the sight does look evil. Kulik is overwhelmed. This is like nothing he has ever seen, or even imagined. The devastation spreads farther than the eye can see. The earth is pockmarked by holes, and waves and folds upon itself. The men search for the center of the area, for where the meteorite must lay. But there is no meteorite. Nor is there a crater that a meteorite would leave. What can have caused this devastation?

Tungus natives, in a photograph taken around the time of the explosion.

The expedition returns home, and Kulik's reports arouse the interest of scientists around the world. They send Kulik their records of the atmospheric and seismic disturbances at the time of the explosion. Study of the records reveals that the force of the explosion was so great that it had sent shock waves traveling twice around the world. Had the explosion occurred over New York or London, those cities would have been wiped out. How lucky it had happened in empty Siberia! But, if it happened before, it could happen again. And what was "it"? If "it" were a meteorite, where was it? Where was the crater? What had happened here?

Some scientists venture an answer: the meteorite exploded in midair. But further investigation of this theory is stopped by World War II. And Leonid Kulik, the scientist who has spent a large part of his life working on the problem, fights and is captured and dies in a Nazi prisoner-of-war camp in Smolensk.

Kulik's investigations are not neglected, however. At the end of the war, a respected Soviet scientist and author, Alexsander Kazantsev, presents a new theory: the Tunguska explosion, as it is now called, had to have been atomic! Pictures of the explosion site show marked similarities to pictures of the destruction in Hiroshima, and Kazantsev saw that destruction personally shortly after the war. The eyewitness reports from Hiroshima and Nagasaki sound like those from the Tunguska explosion. The reports of great heat that puzzled Kulik would fit with an atomic explosion. Calculations of the dimensions of the damaged region show that the explosion had to have been about two miles above ground and up to 1,500 times greater than at Hiroshima, with a temperature of tens of millions of degrees. Only nuclear fission could have attained such temperatures.

Expeditions armed with knowledge of nuclear physics investigate the Tunguska site. Above-normal radiation levels mark the site, particularly close to its center. While Soviet H-bomb testing to the north may affect the readings, then it would be expected that readings in the north rather than in the center would be higher. Glasslike particles of fused minerals suggest atomic radiation, as do the burn patterns of trees and forest. Genetic changes in plants in the area and accelerated growth in new trees are also typical of atomic radiation sites. There seems to have been no radiation poisoning among the natives, although the skin disease of the reindeer reported at the time could have been caused by radiation.

But an atomic bomb in 1908?

Some try to explain the Tunguska explosion with natural phenomena. Theories of antimatter and black holes are advanced. A report in the United States rejects the antimatter theory. An explosion caused by antimatter would have shown absorption of radioactive carbon 14 or radioactive carbon dioxide, and the trees in the Tunguska explosion do not. Two scientists at the University of Texas propose their theory: a dense black hole which hit the planet Earth and passed right through it like a bullet. Very little is known about the behavior of black holes, and other scientists have reservations about this theory. And aerial photographs of the site show an oval pattern of destruction, not circular as would be expected from a natural body. Some sort of oval container must have held the explosive. Droplets of fused metals and extraterrestrial materials found at the site are explained as remnants of the container—which these scientists say was probably a spaceship!

A Soviet airplane designer maps the passage of the Tunguska fireball, using the collection of eyewitness reports marking its trail from Mongolia's Gobi Desert. He discovers that its progress, while faster than the speed of sound, is slower than that of any natural body falling from the heavens. Its speed was about that of a high-altitude supersonic plane. Its direction also seems to have undergone a marked change from northeast to northwest. Only a controlled object could do this. But how reliable are the eyewitness reports?

The site of the devastation hasn't changed much, and it can be clearly seen from the air. Still, no one knows its cause. None of the explanations satisfy everyone. Perhaps future technology will reveal the true nature of the Tunguska explosion. Meanwhile, scientific papers, magazine articles, books, and films reflect the continuing interest of the Soviets in the mystery of what happened that June day in 1908 in Siberia.

Evil   spirits—meteorite—comet—antimatter—black   hole—
spaceship—the theories are terrifying and at the same time
wondrous.

The Tunguska explosion seems to mirror the contradic-
tions, the mystery, and the terror of one of the most awesome
places on Earth: Siberia.

2

The Huns, the Horde,
and the Terrible

THE URAL MOUNTAINS are Siberia's western boundary, and the gateway between Europe and Asia. The Urals are rich in minerals—platinum, uranium, gold, silver, coal, iron, chrome, nickel, magnesium, molybdenum, zinc, lead, copper, and precious stones like emeralds, sapphires, topazes, tourmalines, aquamarines, and more. Generations of students in Soviet schools still joke that if you are asked to name the source of any mineral, always answer "the Urals," for it's almost sure to be there.

The wealth of the Urals is not in its minerals alone but in its many industries using these minerals. The largest iron and steel plant in the Soviet Union is on the Siberian side of the Urals. Built by forced labor and with the technical assistance of American experts, the plant was the focus for the founding of one of Siberia's major cities, Magnitogorsk.

The Urals are very rich and very old. They are not very

Native tent on the tundra, much like the tents of prehistoric times.

high, for the winds and storms of the ages have worn their tops into dust, although they get somewhat steeper toward the north. But many thousands of years ago, when the Urals were higher, it was not their minerals that drew human beings to them. The Urals were a gateway to the West for Neanderthal and then Cro-Magnon groups known as Yenisei Man—after the great Yenisei River in Central Siberia. These early people were probably the forebears of the Slavs, who intermarried with Finnish tribes. The Eastern Slav tribes formed into the city-state of Kiev, the core of what would become Russia. Invasions and conquests divided the Eastern Slavs into three culturally and politically different people—the Great Russians, the Belorussians, and the Ukrainians. All three were responsible for the development of the country and are known today as the Eastern Slav Family. Like most families, the three tend to

Woolly mammoth: a partially excavated specimen, and as it was reconstructed for a museum exhibit.

squabble about their places, contributions, and individuality, but present a united front to other peoples who populated Russia.

(Other Cro-Magnon groups in Siberia eventually crossed a bridge of land that rose between Siberia and America during the several Ice Ages when the sea froze, making its volume smaller. These Siberian immigrants to the North American continent were the people who came to be known as Eskimos and Indians.)

These migrations took thousands of years, as hunters followed game and searched for the long, slender, curved ivory tusks of the great woolly mammoth, an elephantlike species with a heavy, hairy coat. The mammoth roamed the earth in Pleistocene times, the era of the great Ice Ages, and has been extinct since then. But four complete specimens and about forty partial specimens and many thousands of tusks have been found in northern Siberia. Some very brave natives of recent times tasted the meat and pronounced it good, preserved for thousands and thousands of years without harm in Mother Nature's deep freeze.

Mammoths are not the only ancient finds in Siberia. Yenisei man left drawings and writings on rocks and mammoth ivory, and ivory sculptures, and artifacts. Tombs with fully harnessed and decorated skeletons of horses, furs, wools and silks, garments, saddles, embalmed bodies, and jewels and gold ornaments have also survived and show the influence of many civilizations: Scythian, Assyrian, Chaldaean, Babylonian, Roman, Greek, Viking. It was a group of these Vikings called the Rus who gave Russia its name.

By the year 1030, hunters from the city-states of Novgorod and Muscovy (in which lay the tiny village of Moscow) were regularly crossing the Ural Mountains into Siberia, moving east to the Ob River in their search for mammoth ivory and furs. Fur-bearing animals were highly prized, and hunters continually braved the inhospitable north of Siberia for this "soft gold" that made them wealthy.

The Urals gate between continents swung both ways. Out of Siberia came waves of invasion that swamped Europe and Central Asia. First came the Goths, and then, in the fifth century, Attila the Hun left his homeland around Lake Baikal in central Siberia, combined his tribes with others, and swept through the Balkans and Gaul, of which France and Italy were then part. Some say that the name "Siberia" came from one of these early tribes, the "Savirs." (There are other sources that say Siberia was called Yugra at least until the eleventh century, or that the name came from the eastern Mongol city of Sybir, although the two were known separately on early maps. Still others say it was just a chance joining of sounds, or an obscure native word. And so we have another Siberian mystery!)

In the first quarter of the thirteenth century, Genghis Khan and his Mongol tribesmen gathered with other Siberian tribes, including the Tatars, and thundered out of Siberia to take on half the known world. They conquered China, Turkestan, Afghanistan, Persia, and the city-states of Russia to amass one of the greatest empires the world has ever seen.

After Genghis Khan died, his empire came to be known as the Golden Horde. The Horde spread its conquests and its cruelties, killing millions, many by torture. The last leader of the Golden Horde, Tamerlane, had pyramids built of the skulls of his victims as he conquered the cities of India. His pyramid in Delhi was formed from 80,000 skulls.

Siberia was not the only breeding ground for savagery. On the European side of the Urals, the barbarous and often mad princes of the Russian city-states were continually invading and fighting one another. There were Viking attacks from the north, battles with the Poles and other peoples in the west, and wars with the Turks and Persians in the south. Savagery knew no bounds, and imprinted itself on Russian civilization.

In 1300, a Prince of Muscovy, Dmitri Donskoy, introduced firearms to his men and brought about the first defeat of the Golden Horde. This was not enough to break up the empire, however. That took another hundred years. By then, the ruling Mongols were a minority, seriously outnumbered by the rank-and-file Tatar members of the Horde. Their authority was eroded. And when the Mongols, once tolerant of all religions, adopted Islam as the official religion of the Golden Horde, their men deserted in large numbers. Soon there were not enough men to control the widespread empire. The Horde was being weakened further as Mongol and Tatar members of powerful families married into great Slav families and lost their interest in war for war's sake. When Tamerlane died in 1405 there was no one strong enough to command, and the Horde broke up into the separate khanates of Crimea, Kazan, Astrakhan, and Siberia.

The khanates continued to demand tribute from the Russian princes. Finally, Ivan III, Grand Prince of Muscovy, fresh from his conquests of the city-states of Novgorod, Tver, and several other principalities, refused to pay. Probably to his surprise, the khans made no attempt to force him. Ivan was so pleased at his power that he declared himself the first czar, Czar of Muscovy; the word "czar" he derived from "Caesar."

Now it was the khans who paid tribute. But by the middle 1500s, they, too, refused to pay. They picked the wrong man to defy. He was Ivan IV, known as "Ivan the Terrible." A Czar of Muscovy, he had united the Russian city-states under his rule and had become the first Czar of Russia. Ivan wanted his tribute and when he didn't get it, he went out and conquered the khanates of Kazan and Astrakhan. When Kuchum Khan of the khanate of Siberia refused to pay his annual tribute of furs, Ivan, who was growing increasingly insane, became madder than usual. He had a lot of other things on his mind at the time, many of them obsessions of persecution, but he was no fool. He let the wealthy and powerful merchant family, the Stroganovs, do his work for him. The Stroganovs had great estates west of the Urals. Ivan simply issued a *ukase*, a royal decree, giving the Stroganovs a great estate east of the Urals— in Siberia. Of course, Siberia did not belong to Russia, and the lands weren't Ivan's to give. But once they were taken by the Stroganovs, the lands would never again belong to the Khan of Siberia.

The Stroganovs called on their Cossacks. Cossacks were formerly the hard-riding, hard-fighting frontier troops of the Crimean Khanate. When the khanate was taken over by the Turks in 1478, the Cossacks settled along the rivers of Russia and became the Volga Cossacks, the Don Cossacks, and so forth. The Cossacks were a class to themselves, and their ranks were soon enlarged by members of the peasant class escaping one persecution or another. The Cossacks elected their own leaders and lived by their own laws. Cossack brigands terrorized the countryside, killing and raping and looting. Eventually, the only way the czars could control them was by enlisting them in the royal service. Armies of Cossacks hired themselves out to great landowners like the Stroganovs to protect their estates or guard their towns or keep their peasants in line. Idle Cossacks made a lot of trouble, so the Stroganovs were happy to give the 5,000 or so Cossacks on their estates the job of getting those furs—and Siberia—for the Czar.

A Cossack soldier, about 1860.

The Cossack *hetman* or leader, Yermak, was sitting on the Stroganov estates because he was more or less hiding from the wrath of the Czar over some transgression or other. When he was asked to move on the Khan of Siberia, he knew he would be doing a favor for the Czar as well as the Stroganovs, a favor that would surely bring him rich rewards as well as relief from the royal displeasure. Yermak negotiated a winter wait-over in the warmth and abundance of Stroganov hospitality, and in the spring of 1581 crossed the Urals into Siberia.

Most of Yermak's men had deserted during the winter, less than enthusiastic about coming up against the remnants of the Golden Horde. But Yermak had something that was almost better than men in those days of bows and arrows: he had three cannon. And Yermak didn't know it, but Kuchum Khan was also having trouble holding his army together. His men were held by old and complicated ties of blood and marriage and revenge dating back hundreds of years. Those ties were unraveling, and many of the men were tired of being conquerors or even of being warriors. They were still superior in numbers to Yermak's men, now down to well under a thousand, but in the end Cossack guns prevailed. A few last survivors of the Horde lost themselves in the *taiga,* and Yermak made himself the Czar of Siberia.

No one minded in the least. Ivan graciously accepted Yermak's gifts of furs—and Siberia—and allowed Yermak his title. With no effort at all, Ivan the Terrible now ruled over a Russia that had quadrupled in size. The Stroganovs also won. The Czar gave them more estates in more civilized parts of Russia. Yermak, however, was not to enjoy his czardom for long. He died, probably by drowning in Siberia's Irtysh River, possibly at the hands of vengeful Tatars, possibly because, as legend has it, he tried to ford the river while wearing the silver armor sent to him by Ivan the Terrible.

3

The Wild, Wild East

THE URALS GATEWAY swung wide once again, but now the movement was into Siberia as Cossacks and fugitive criminals and hunters and traders and men with itchy feet made their way east. These were the *promyshlenniki,* the pioneers who opened Siberia. Their way was bloody and cruel. The conquest of the Siberian natives was not peaceful, as is sometimes claimed, but there was less bloodshed than there was to be when the American West was settled, because the fight was more one-sided. The natives of Siberia had long before lost their will to fight after centuries of doing little else under the khans and the Golden Horde. They fell easy victim or fled farther north into less hospitable land where no one followed. There were no huge movements of settlers into Siberia, so retreat was feasible. Retreat may seem peaceful, but it is painful, and the natives suffered as the Russians moved slowly eastward, sweeping them away as they went.

Although the weather was better to the south, the rivers kept the *promyshlenniki* to the north. Siberia's great rivers flow north, and the rowing of boats or poling of rafts was much easier downstream. Then, too, hunting was better in the colder north where animals pelts were heavier. So the men zigzagged along, connecting with tributary west-east rivers or portaging their boats, carrying them overland until they reached the next river. Portages were easy, for Siberia has many thousands of rivers. It was not until 1643 that travel to the more hospitable south was opened. The Cossack Poyarkov and his men traveled up the Lena River instead of down, and after a journey of months moved on to the Amur River. The Amur flows in a southeasterly direction for almost half its length, then turns sharply north, emptying into the Strait of Tatar, an extension of the Pacific. But Poyarkov was not interested in following the Amur when it turned north. For all he knew, the journey might take so long he could never get back. Instead he went back by way of the mountains, opening a route there for future travelers. Few travelers came.

Cossacks were sent into Siberia to police the *promyshlenniki* and help take the land from the natives. They built fortresses called *ostrogs* within easy riding distance of one another. Around them small towns grew, as Cossack wives joined their husbands, as hunters married native women and set up homes. The first Russian town in Siberia was Tobolsk, on the Tobol River where it connects with the Irtysh, a natural enough setting in a country where travel was by river. On the Yenisei they built Krasnoyarsk and Yeneseisk, opening a vast, fortified trading post. On the Lena, they founded Yakutsk; on the Tom River, Tomsk. On the Angara River northwest of Lake Baikal, the deepest lake in the world, they built Irkutsk. All were to become great cities in time. But their growth was slow. Few

Remains of the ostrog *(left) at Omsk.*

settlers followed in the wake of the *promyshlenniki,* yet the settlement of Siberia was urgent to prevent other countries—China, Mongolia, Korea, Afghanistan—from moving in from the south.

Settlers did not come for several very good reasons. The trip was long and difficult. The climate was certainly no inducement. The weather is harder in Siberia than on the European side of the Urals. Mountains on the west, south, and east of Siberia hold in the icy north winds from the Arctic like coffee in a cup; warming southern winds are kept out of the cup by the saucerlike mountain ranges between China and Siberia. Western Siberia, which was as far as settlers could go in those days, was wet, swampy, and covered with dense thicket, although in the south settlers would find an extension of Russia's famed black earth belt ripe for planting. And farther east there was the central Siberian plateau, the *steppes.* But even when they could reach these places, even when they

Frozen land turns to bog in Siberian summers.

were offered free land and no taxes and exemption from
military service, even then the people did not emigrate. Even
if Siberia were their idea of the promised land, they could not
get there, for most of them were enslaved.

Slavery had been legal in Russia from the earliest times,
but the peasant class, those who worked the land, had been
relatively free. Some peasants, however, bound themselves to
landlords—agreed to work for little or no pay in return for
loans of money. They became *serfs*. Many countries had bound
people, usually sentenced under the laws of the times to one
kind of servitude or another, and some early immigrants to
America bound themselves for a period of perhaps five or
seven years to buy their passage over. But in Russia, loans of
money could only be repaid by money, and serfs could never
earn enough hard cash—that's why they bound themselves in
the first place. So these people were bound for life, and their

debts and status as serfs were inherited by their descendants.

Serfdom was not widespread until the 1500s. It was then that Ivan the Terrible created a new aristocracy, men like the Stroganovs to whom he gave land in return for their services to the crown. Land without workers was useless, so laws were passed binding the peasants to the villages they lived in, making them serfs. In 1649, serfdom was made a state institution like slavery, and serfs became the actual property of the landlords. It was impossible to distinguish between slaves and serfs, and, in fact, Catherine the Great was to combine the two groups. She decided to call them all serfs, but slaves would have been the more correct term.

Serfs were bought and sold and traded and used as their masters desired. A landowner usually had so many serfs that he could not manage them directly. The villages each had their own councils called *mirs*, usually composed of the older men, who represented the peasants and also administered the wishes of the landowner. The *mir* collected the taxes that these poor enslaved people had to pay, resolved disputes, redistributed housing and the land that had to be worked, and saw to it that the young men went off on the military service they had to perform. This gave the *mirs* much power over the individual and opened the way to bribery and mismanagement of land and people. But the *mirs* gave the people some form of self-government.

Northern Russian and Siberia did not have serfdom, because there were no large landowners there. However, whole villages of serfs were relocated from the rest of Russia to Siberia at the order of the czars who saw the serfs as one solution to their problem of settlement of Siberia. The owner of thousands of serfs—and there were many with such large holdings—could easily part with hundreds to curry favor with the Czar.

Map drawn under the direction of Boris Godunov.

NOVA ZEMLA

MANSKOY MORE

Lampas
Tarck hoek

Beier ostroef

SAMOIEDA

Tingoeſi.

BAIDA

obdora

SIBIRIA

Iugoria

Con dora

Pega orda.

Permia

TARTA

RIÆ

Wiatka

CAZAN

Ceremiſſi ſupeꝛi
ſi dicti quod montana incolunt
Ceremis commune eſt
Tartarorum Regni Caſani

MORDWA

PARS.

BOCHAR

OPEN SIS.

PERE C.

IVRMEN

TVRCMEN

CALMVCKI.

CARATAN
SCA
ORDO

RUSSIA

ASTRACAN.

Tanais, nunc Don flu.
ut maius inter Europæos et Uſios

PETIGORI.

MARE CASPIVM, quod

Ruſſi   vocant

GVALEN TSCHA MORE

Aſtrachan

GILAN REGIO.

PERSIÆ CONFINIA.

ZIRPHANSCKA REGIO.

ARMENIA

Iveria ſive Gruſinæ Imperium

ARCHANGELSCKAGORODA

No one cared that these people might not want to go or might not be able to make it on their own in the impossibly hard conditions in Siberia. There was no one to help them in that wilderness, no one to teach them what to do when the scant knowledge they had acquired as serfs failed them, and great numbers did not survive the trip or the resettlement.

Instead of a new land that promised opportunity, Siberia promised only hardship; instead of freedom, Siberia offered exile.

Siberia had been made a place of exile only a few years after Yermak had presented it to Ivan the Terrible. The first exile to Siberia was a bell. But first it had its tongue cut out.

The man responsible was Boris Godunov, Ivan's son-in-law and advisor. When Ivan died and his young son, Feodor, became Czar, Godunov was made regent. Then Feodor's brother and heir, the Czarevitch Dmitri, was murdered in the fortress at Uglich. The town bell had tolled Dmitri's death, whether joyously or mournfully is not known, but obviously it should have remained silent. Along with the bell, thirty families of Uglich were also sent into exile, just for having been there. Actually, Godunov himself was suspected of having a hand in Dmitri's death, particularly when Czar Feodor also died and the way was clear for Godunov to be made Czar.

The accession of Boris Godunov to the throne in 1598 brought the "Time of Troubles" to Russia. The people did not like Godunov and were in a state of unrest. The Cossacks were running out of control, Sweden and Poland both invaded, and numerous pretenders to the throne marched on Moscow. At least four claimed to be Dmitri risen from the dead, and one was a prince of Poland bent on annexing Russia. When Boris Godunov died in the midst of all this, Russia found itself with no less than five czars on its hands. Chaos reigned until a volunteer army expelled the invaders and a Romanov prince, Mikhail, was elected by the nobles to assume the throne in 1613. Related to the wife of Ivan the Terrible, he at least had some legitimate claim to the monarchy. The Romanov dynasty was to rule until the Russian Revolution of 1917, and one of the ways the Romanovs maintained power over those three hundred years was to use the Siberian exile system freely.

4

Expanding Frontiers

I T WOULD TAKE a lot of exiles to fill up the Siberia that was expanding eastward and south. Fortunately, her neighbors to the south showed no interest in claiming Siberian territory. But then the Russians decided that the southern border of Siberia belonged at the Amur River by right of exploration. And the Chinese saw the Amur River as inside their country.

Poyarkov's exploration of the section of the Amur River that flowed south had been followed by further charting by another explorer, Yerofei Khabarov. Khabarov (after whom the city of Khabarovsk in Far Eastern Siberia is named) was a true Cossack. He and his men burned, killed, tortured, mutilated, and enslaved wherever they went. They even harried the Chinese, although expressly warned against provoking an incident. After all, borders are delicate things, particularly when they are being extended by one party at the expense of another.

Russia did not want a war with China. China's might was legendary. Besides, it would take years for Russia to move troops into the remote Amur area. China did not want war either. Their might was more legend than fact, and they, too, would have trouble moving troops to their northern border—but Russia did not know that. Instead of going to war, the two countries sat down at the treaty table and worked out a peaceful settlement of where the Russian-Chinese border lay.

The Treaty of Nerchinsk of 1689 was China's first treaty with a European power. The results did not make Russia happy. The border was set to the north of the Amur, at the Shilka River and across the Stanovoy mountain range, stopping at the Sea of Okhotsk, an inlet of the Pacific Ocean, because the land beyond that was uncharted.

Charting was only a matter of time, for in this same year, 1689, Czar Peter I assumed active control of the government, and Peter had a monumental thirst for knowledge. Peter and his half-brother, Ivan, had been joint czars for some seven years. But Ivan was retarded and Peter was too young to reign, so the country had been ruled by a regent, their sister, Sophia Alexeyevna. Now Peter, only seventeen, had succeeded in overthrowing Sophia. Ivan took no part in the government, and he and Peter coexisted peacefully as joint czars until Ivan's death in 1696. Peter, known to history as the Great, modernized Russia and brought it into the forefront of European nations. He fostered the search for information of all kinds, and he organized and reorganized the tools of government.

In Siberia, Peter started a system of registration and control of exiles and other settlers to spread them out more equably. (Government being as cumbersome as it was, the system took almost 150 years to work properly.) He also provided for more efficient administration of Russia's provinces, of which Siberia was one. A Prince Gagarin was appointed as the first chief administrator or Governor-General of Siberia. The prince promptly proceeded to loot the treasury. His display of wealth was so outrageous, even in a country known for the fabulous riches and life-styles of its aristocracy, that the Czar ordered him investigated. The result was a trial, flogging, and hanging. After all, Gagarin could not very well be sentenced to exile in Siberia!

Peter's interest in Siberia was not limited to administration. He also ordered the exploration and mapping of northeast Siberia, with a particular eye to finding out if the continents of Asia and America were joined in the far north as native tales seemed to indicate. If so, Peter, who had turned the country into an empire and now ruled as the first Emperor of All Russia, could extend his empire to a third continent— America.

Peter didn't know it, but the answer to his question was already in the government's files in Siberia. A seafarer, Semeon Ivanovich Dezhnev, had sailed between the continents in 1648. He had given his report to the authorities in Irkutsk, who promptly filed it away and forgot it, unaware of its importance. So Vitus Bering, a Dane in Russian service, was sent by the Czar to the waters that are now the Bering Strait and the Bering Sea instead of the Dezhnev. Dezhnev didn't get his name on the map until 1898, when East Cape, the northeasternmost point of the Asian continent, was renamed Cape Dezhnev.

Bering almost didn't make it into the geography books either. He set sail in 1728, after spending three years of hauling men and supplies overland through Siberia to the Pacific and readying his ship. Then he didn't see the American continent when he finally sailed by it. He couldn't see anything; the weather, as always, was foggy and stormy. He tried a second time, but was blown off course and accidentally discovered the southern route around the peninsula of Kamchatka. Bering went back to Russia's new capital, St. Petersburg, without an answer for Peter the Great. It didn't matter. By this time it was 1730 and Peter had been dead for five years.

Interest in northeast Siberia did not die with Peter, however. Bering set up a huge mapping expedition of the high Arctic territory, the Great Northern Expedition, that proved very successful though of little immediate importance. Only explorers cared to go to northeast Siberia and no one needed its vast supply of minerals in those days.

Then, after ten years of preparation, Bering took off in 1741 for another try at finding America. This time he was successful. He not only saw the continent—at Alaska—but landed a party of scientists there. They had barely looked around when they were ordered back on board ship. Their rage and frustration at not being able to investigate the new land after all those years of preparation can only be imagined. But the ship's crew was riddled with scurvy, and only a few were strong enough to man the sails for the voyage home. Bering knew it would be fatal to stay any longer. He himself was mortally ill with scurvy and was to die on a little island where the ill-fated ship was wrecked. The island was named after him, and the chain of islands to which it belonged was named the Komandorski or Commander Islands for Bering's rank of Captain Commander. The strait dividing Asia and America was named the Bering Strait, and the sea above it the Bering Sea. And two members of his expedition, Dmitri Laptev and Khariton Laptev, were to be honored in geography books when, some two centuries later, the Nordenskjöld Sea was Russianized into the Laptev Sea. (The Laptev Sea borders the New Siberian Islands discovered in the 1760s by a merchant

An island in the Bering Sea today habitated by humans as well as seals.

named Liakhov, so Liakhov Sea might have been more accurate if a Russian name was imperative. But Liakhov was not lucky geographically.)

A second ship had started out with Bering but somehow had become separated from the command ship. The crew had continued on alone and had discovered the Aleutian Islands, bringing back sea otter skins that sent the *promyshlenniki* out in droves.

Alaska and the Aleutians tantalized the Russians. There they were, just a few miles from Siberia, and neither the Spanish to the south in the land of California nor the British in Canada seemed to want them. The *promyshlenniki* were bringing back fortunes in skins—and leaving behind a deep and abiding hatred in the natives for their cruelty. A Russian merchant named Gregori Ivanovich Shelikov, rich on Siberian furs, was determined to get richer on Alaskan furs, but not as one of the *promyshlenniki*. He wanted to form a great empire-building company like those of the Dutch and English. He went to Alaska, and in 1784 founded the first permanent nonnative settlement on Kodiak Island, separated from the mainland by what he called Shelikov Strait. Shelikov returned to Russia, sending Alexander Baranov to rule his Alaskan settlements. Baranov established New Archangel, now Sitka, on Baranov Island (what else?) and sent out ships to explore the Aleutians. One of the ships was commanded by Gerasim Pribilof, who discovered a group of four islands, the Pribilof Islands (what else?), now famous as a major breeding place of the seal.

Shelikov had a son-in-law, Captain Nicolai Petrovich Rezanov, who came from Siberia and was one of the many favorites of Catherine the Great, Czarina and Empress of All Russia. Rezanov spoke to Catherine, and Shelikov and he were given a charter in 1799 establishing the Russian American Company (not to be confused with the Russia or Muscovy Company, the first of the stockholders' companies, formed in the 1500s by Sebastian Cabot to explore and trade in Russia and find a Northeast Passage to China and India). The Russian American Company was to develop trade and establish the Russian empire in Alaska and the Aleutian and Kurile islands. Of course, they were already doing this, but now they had official standing. Baranov extended trade and settlement farther and farther south, until Russian America reached almost to San Francisco.

Rezanov meanwhile had persuaded the new czar, Alexander II, to send two Russian ships around the world on a trade mission. He himself went to Japan, but after six months of waiting was sent back without an interview and with the gifts he had brought from the Czar. Japan was closed. Rezanov went on to Sitka, reaching there in 1805, and found its people close to starvation. There was food to be had in the south, and Rezanov went to San Francisco to negotiate with the commandant of the Spanish territory in California. There he found that all trade from California had to go through Spain, so the supplies Sitka desperately needed would have to go round the world rather than simply up the coast. This obviously would not do, and it took all of Rezanov's persuasive powers to get the food. His powers had worked on an empress and now they worked on the Governor-General of Spanish America. The food would be sent directly to Russian America, marking the beginning of trade between nations on the Pacific coast.

Rezanov's persuasive powers were helped by the powers of romance. His wife had died, and now Rezanov fell in love with Doña Concepción, daughter of the Spanish commandant. The two became engaged but could not marry because of their different religions. Dispensations were needed from the Czar, the head of the Russian Orthodox Church, and from the Pope, head of the Roman Catholic Church. Rezanov raced back to Sitka with the food, then started for St. Petersburg and Rome. On the way he stopped off quickly at the Kuriles and Sakhalin Island to give the natives there a coin and a document saying they were now part of the Russian empire (which could have confused them if they recognized the language because the Japanese had made them part of their empire also). But in Siberia death overtook the gallant Rezanov in 1807. Doña Concepción waited—and then became a nun. She did not find out what had happened to her fiancé until thirty-seven years after he had died.

As the years passed, and the United States found its way to the Pacific and the British became more protective of the rights of Canada, Russian America began to feel threatened. The Czar issued a *ukase* forbidding foreign ships to encroach upon Alaska and the Aleutians. Washington invoked the Monroe Doctrine and issued a warning about foreign powers encroaching upon American territory. Russia reconsidered her position. Profits from Russian America were not spectacular, certainly not good enough to risk a war, which Russia could hardly hope to win. Her supply lines could not stretch across Siberia and the Pacific to reach a continent halfway around the world. Russia's ambassadors recommended a discreet withdrawal, possibly turning the territory over to the Americans as a gracious gift. In the end, they sold Russian America to the United States in 1867, happy to get the $7,200,000 purchase price negotiated with Secretary of State William H. Seward, and turned back to Siberia as a base for trade in the Pacific.

5

Of Wars and Back Doors

IT HAD BEEN easier for Russia to trade from the American side of the Pacific than the Siberian side. There was no trade in Far Eastern Siberia. Reaching there was so difficult that few *promyshlenniki* and Cossacks had come that way to develop trading posts, although it was a place of exile. Iced-in much of the year, Kamchatka Peninsula saw little boat traffic. But by the time she sold Alaska, Russia had found a river route to the Pacific that opened up Far Eastern Siberia for development.

In 1853, Russia and the Ottoman Empire had gone to war—the Crimean War—after Russia had seized two vassal states of the Empire. Russia's real goal was control of the Black Sea so that she could reach the oceans more easily. Turkey, part of the Ottoman Empire, regarded the Black Sea as her private lake. Great Britain, France, and Sardinia had joined in the fight against Russia, much to her surprise. British and

The main street of a town in Siberia around 1860 (drawing).

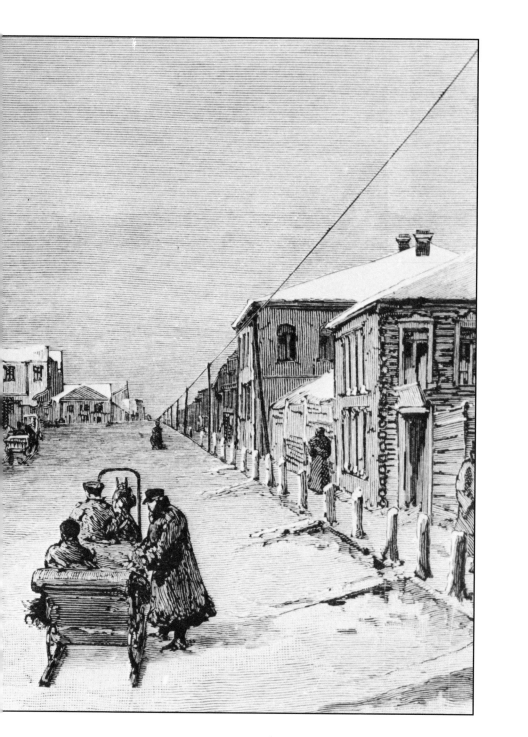

French naval ships in the Pacific could easily debark troops into her back door in Siberia, and Russia could not defend against such an invasion. Bringing up troops, equipment, and supplies overland to close that back door would take months. Nor could Russia afford to divert troops from the fighting at her front door in the Crimea to wait in Siberia for an invasion that might never come.

It was clear that Russia had to develop a faster route across Siberia to the Pacific, a river route. She had to move troops more rapidly in times of war, and she also had to have a way to move settlers across Siberia more easily so as to secure Russia's claim to the land and to develop its economic potential.

The Amur River seemed to be the only answer, but the Amur belonged to China by the Treaty of Nerchinsk. And Russia's foreign service, busy with the war in the Crimea and anxious to avoid war with China, assured Czar Nicholas I that the Amur would not lead to the Pacific anyway. They insisted that the Strait of Tatar, the link between the river and the sea, was not navigable. There seemed to be no answer after all.

The Governor-General of Siberia, Nicholas Nicholayevitch Muraviev, refused to accept that. Near the end of the Crimean War, Muraviev loaded 1,000 troops and provisions on huge rafts and set off down the Amur. The Chinese made one feeble attempt to stop them, but they were easily bluffed with the mention of a nearby, purely imaginary, army. The Russians were allowed to continue on without interference, and arrived triumphantly at the Pacific in time to turn away a small enemy sea patrol. The Amur was proven navigable all the way to the sea. But the Amur was not Russian.

Muraviev was determined to win the Amur once and for all, a determination strengthened by Russia's humiliating loss of the Crimean War. Down the river he went again, this time in a military convoy of three powered boats. And this time an envoy from the Chinese Emperor was waiting to remind the Russians that they were on Chinese territory. Muraviev mentioned his imaginary army beyond the horizon. The envoy was as good at bluffing as Muraviev, and countered with his own imaginary army. But Muraviev had one better, and very real, argument. China and Britain were engaged in the Opium Wars at the time, 1860, and Muraviev pointed out that in the age of steamboats, travel upstream was as easy as down. The British navy could come up the Amur and attack China's unfortified northern back door just as easily as Siberia's back door. But here were three Russian boats, ready to defend the entryway for the Chinese as well as themselves. The envoy was quick to take the point, and gave the Amur River into the safekeeping of Russia. In return, the two men agreed to a modification of the Chinese-Siberian border. The Amur was to belong entirely to Russia until it turned north at its junction with China's Ussuri River. From there to the Strait of Tatar and the Pacific, the Amur would be China's and Russia's jointly. The peninsula between the Amur and the Strait would also be held jointly.

A sizable chunk of territory was added to Siberia by this agreement. But even so, Muraviev had no intention of honoring the parts that called for joint ownership, particularly of that peninsula with the port of Vladivostok at the tip. Vladivostok was Russian by right of exploration, and Russia needed that Pacific outpost. No problem. Muraviev knew that China had no way to get her troops north fast enough to cause him any trouble. After all, that was why China had given Russia the rights to the Amur in the first place. So, when he was far enough away, Muraviev simply sent a messenger informing the hapless Chinese that they were out of the picture, that their exceedingly brief joint holdings were no longer joint but were Russia's alone. In one fell swoop, Muraviev had secured the Maritime Territory, the extension of Siberia's southern border, and the Amur River for trade and a water route to the Pacific.

Understandably, Muraviev was made Count Muraviev-Amurski by a grateful Czar.

China was not happy at the shrinking of her northern border, but she was more unhappy about the Russian assumption of the Amur. When the Chinese rebelled against Westerners and Western influence in the Boxer Rebellion (1898–1900), tension rose along the Amur River border. Although Siberia is Asian, it was—and is—populated almost entirely by people of European descent. At Blagoveshchensk, the largest Russian town on the Amur, the Chinese fired on a Russian convoy. Their aim was deplorable, and shells killed some fifteen citizens in the town. The Russians, particularly the violent Amur Cossacks, sought revenge. When the Boxer Rebellion had begun, the Chinese who worked and lived in Blagoveshchensk had been assured they were safe, but now they were rounded up and slaughtered by the Cossacks. Good Russian citizens felt it was their duty to their country to turn in every Chinese, even friends and servants, for the Cossacks to kill. The killings were not for vengeance only. They were racially and economically motivated as well. The slaughter wiped out Russian debts to Chinese merchants and moneylenders, and confiscation of Chinese property made some citizens of Blagoveshchensk rich. So the slaughter spread. Thousands of Chinese, many of them mothers with young children, were herded to the banks of the Amur and told to swim to the other side. Few were strong enough, and those few who did not drown found themselves being gunned down by the Chinese

The Amur River at Blagoveshchensk at the time of the massacre of the Chinese.

as Russians and Russian sympathizers. Ten to fifteen thousand people died in that border conflict. Nobody could make an accurate count because too many bodies were swept away down the Amur River.

   (The dispute over the Amur River continues to this day. In the 1960s, frequent military skirmishes over strategic islands in the river resulted in many deaths. In 1987, talks opened in Moscow to settle the issue. The Amur has already suffered a curious amputation; on some new maps its northward course has taken on the name of its tributary, the Ussuri River. This seems to strengthen Chinese claims, since the Ussuri rises out of China. China wants the Muraviev 1860 agreement torn up as "unequal." Of course it wasn't the treaty that was unequal, it was its execution by Muraviev.)

A troika (drawing).

The Amur proved a good route for Russian-Chinese trade but not for bringing in more population to develop Far Eastern Siberia, and merchants weren't reaping the profits they had hoped for. Besides, the Amur was too far south. Cities and towns were developing along the old Cossack routes farther north. People there needed better transportation to bring in goods and they needed markets to sell their wares and surplus produce—the farms in parts of Siberia were proving surprisingly productive.

There was only one main road west to east through Siberia, the Moscow Road or Track. It was a good road, surfaced, and sixteen carriages wide. (Russia always believed in wide roads, even when nothing travels them.) The few north-south roads were not so well developed, but all the tracks had post-houses at easy stages for renting or buying conveyances, changing horses, and getting food or a night's sleep. Carriages or sleighs in winter moved speedily, usually drawn by three horses—Russia's famous *troika*. Passengers sat on cushions and luggage and held on for dear life as carriages bounced madly at what seemed like wild speed. Although winter travel was brutally cold, the ride was smoother in sleighs, and the sleighs were so spacious that passengers could sleep on the floor alongside a small stove to keep them warm. Rivers were turned into roads of ice, so ferries or fording at shallow points could be avoided. Still, travel through Siberia took months, and a lot of money. Siberia could never develop until a better system of transportation was available.

The answer to Siberia's dilemma lay in America. A railroad had spanned the United States in 1869 and opened that country to development. Count Muraviev-Amurski and others tried to convince the Czar and his advisors that Siberia, too, needed a railway. There was much talk but little action, until a great famine broke out in the east of Siberia. Wagonloads of food sent to relieve the stricken area took months to arrive, and the urgent need for a railroad to make eastern Siberia more accessible was finally acknowledged.

The first rails were laid in 1891 for what was to become the longest and one of the greatest railroads in the world: the Trans-Siberian Railway. A shortcut to the Maritime Kray was built across Manchuria under a lease-treaty with the Chinese and completed in 1901. (That it escaped the Boxer Rebellion and retaliation for Blagoveshchensk was undoubtedly a matter of politics and money.) The entire system was completed in 1915—a remarkably short time, considering weather, the terrain, the use of convict labor, and the many hundreds of rivers to be bridged. The bridge crossing the juncture of the Amur

Prisoners at work on the Trans-Siberian Railway.

and Ussuri rivers was the second largest in the world at the time.

But long before the Railway was finished, the Russians realized that the one-track, light-rail system they had laid was inadequate. When in 1904–05 Russia had to move troops and supplies through Siberia for still another war, the Russo-Japanese War, the Railway couldn't handle the volume, and repairs and replacements were undertaken quietly, almost secretly.

The Russians did not like to admit that they had made a mistake about the railroad, and the war was another mistake. Czar Nicholas II and a friend had formed a trading company in Korea rather like Shelikov had done in Russian America.

Railway bridge over the great river Ob.

The elegant train depot at Vladivostok, the vital eastern terminus of the Trans-Siberian Railway.

This didn't please the Russian people, who were clamoring for economic and social improvement at home, not in Korea. It didn't please Japan, either. The Russians in Manchuria were bad enough. If they came to Korea as well, Japan could be swamped. She decided to attack first. Her ships bombarded Port Arthur in Manchuria, held by Russia under lease along with the Trans-Siberian right-of-way. The Russians preferred Port Arthur over Vladivostok as a seaport because it was ice-free.

Czar Nicholas welcomed the war. He saw it as an opportunity to unite his grumbling people behind him in a spirit of patriotism and believed that it would take a mere flick of the hand to get rid of little Japan. Instead, Russia suffered a decisive and humiliating defeat. She not only lost the war, she lost the lease to Port Arthur and to the Manchurian link of the Trans-Siberian Railway. They were given to the Japanese by the Treaty of Portsmouth (New Hampshire, USA) mediated by President Theodore Roosevelt. Both the rail link and the port could be and were replaced. But Japan now had a foothold in Manchuria and was to use it to mount a campaign of imperialism in the Far East and Pacific that was not to end until her defeat in World War II. Russia also had to return the southern half of Siberia's Sakhalin Island to Japan. Russia had turned Sakhalin, on the east of the Tatar Strait, into a penal colony, so southern Sakhalin was not much of a loss. The north, rich in gold, Russia managed to keep. Russia might have lost the war, but not the peace.

But Nicholas was on the brink of losing his country. There was no sense of patriotism within the people, only of revolution. They had to fight the wars, they suffered the losses, but they had no say in the conduct of the government. They slaved, and they saw no way out of the state of ignorance and poverty

The Russian Orthodox Church was everywhere in Siberia; even the Trans-Siberian trains had church cars.

Siberian cities were sophisticated as well as primitive. Here, the home of a Russian Orthodox archbishop (top) and the entry hall of a wealthy business-man's home in Irkutsk, about 1860.

in which they were kept. Technically they were no longer serfs. Serfdom had been ended in 1861 when Czar Alexander II issued an Edict of Emancipation as part of his program of Great Reforms to help bring his people out of darkness, but there were many strings attached to the Edict that kept most peasants as bound as before.

A large middle class had formed when the Industrial Revolution brought manufacturing and mechanization to Russia. Among these more educated Russians, joined by some peasants and members of the aristocracy, dozens of revolutionary groups had formed. Every group had a different philosophy, a different idea of how to achieve reform. Some turned to terrorist techniques of assassination and bombing. Alexander II, called the "Czar Liberator" for his Great Reforms, had been assassinated on the very day he had signed a decree giving the people a representative assembly, and the result had been a czar, Alexander III, who had done away with all his father's good works. Instead of improving the people's lot, the revolutionaries had made it worse. Many thousands were forced to flee—to lose themselves in Siberia, to emigrate to America. Many more thousands were sent into Siberian exile. But that only fueled the revolutionary spirit in the people.

These were the people who objected to the involvement of Alexander's son, Czar Nicholas II, in Korea. These were the people who wanted more and better for the laborer, for the peasant, and were organizing into illegal political groups and unions.

The war with Japan only fueled the people's discontent. Then, even as war still raged, a workers' demonstration on a January Sunday in St. Petersburg was fired on by troops. "Bloody Sunday" started the Russian Revolution of 1905. Peasants seized land, workers went on strike, soldiers and sailors mutinied, and armed groups fought in the streets. The first *soviets*, or councils—the Soviets of Workers' Deputies—presented their demands to the government. And they were listened to. Czar Nicholas II had a constitution drawn up and formed a legislative body, the *Duma*, to give the people a voice in government. Most political groups and unions were legalized, and serfdom was really ended. Peasant debts to landlords were remitted, and the peasants were allowed to move from their villages and their *mirs* and even to buy land through a newly created Peasant Land Bank.

By the summer of 1905, the people seemed more content, the disastrous war with Japan was over, and Nicholas II still reigned as Czar and Emperor of All Russia. The Trans-Siberian Railway was bringing thousands of peasants into Siberia. The government offer of free land was still open, though cut back in size to one *dessiatin* (2.7 acres) per man, considered to be all one man could work. The Trans-Siberian Railway undertook the safekeeping of the emigrants, providing them with food and medical care, and building towns for them along the route. A traveler writing of these new Siberian towns told of how they smelled of fresh-cut wood: the wooden houses, many with elaborate wood carving around the lace-curtained windows, strung out in two long rows on either side of the wide wooden plank street with wooden plank sidewalks. The road was not always planked over, however, and then the houses were separated by seas of mud mixed with horse manure and cow dung! But each town had a church, and often a synagogue and sometimes a mosque, and a meetinghall used as a theater.

When the towns beside the railroad stations filled up, newcomers had to accept more remote locations in which to settle. This was bad. Loneliness, difficult weather, the need to travel to trade goods, but most of all, lack of services, equip-

Boards make a rough street over the mud (drawing).

Towns were thrown up near the railway depots.

ment, supplies, and experience combined to cause many failures among the peasant farms. Somehow, these peasants had to find their way back to European Russia. Those who did brought back bitter stories of the hardships of Siberia. Prospective emigrants to Siberia were discouraged, and many went to America instead. America's gain was Siberia's loss.

6

The Allies and the
Revolutionaries

I N 1914, RUSSIA found herself in still another war,
World War I. This time she was on the side of the Allies—
Great Britain and France, and later the Japanese and
Americans, among others—against the Axis powers of Germany, Austro-Hungary, and Turkey. In Siberia, the Trans-
Siberian Railway was trying to move troops and supplies and
civilian necessities both ways at the same time on the same
tracks. No one seemed able to set up proper timetables or
coordinate shipments. Supplies and equipment sent by the
Americans piled up on the docks of Vladivostok; food rotted
at railroad sidings while armies went hungry and men were
sent in to fight without guns.

Czar Nicholas II took over the front-line command of the
war, leaving the Czarina Alexandra as head of the empire. The
Russian people disliked Alexandra. They thought her a German
sympathizer because she had been born a princess of the Grand

Vladivostok at the start of World War I.

Czar Nicholas II

Duchy of Hesse, later part of Germany. Of course, Alexandra was also a grandchild of Britain's Queen Victoria and Prince Albert, but that didn't stop the rumors; so was the hated Kaiser Wilhelm of Germany.

The rumors were baseless, but the facts were far more disturbing. Alexandra had come under the influence of a sinister Siberian peasant professing to be a monk, Grigori Yefimovich Novykh, better known as Rasputin. Uneducated, uncouth, he came to the Russian court in 1905 and insured himself a place there by using his powers of hypnotism and seemingly of clairvoyance. Alexandra believed that Rasputin had saved the life of her son, the Czarevitch Alexei, on several occasions. The young heir to the throne was afflicted with hemophilia, a fatal blood disease active only in males but inherited from their mothers. Alexandra's feelings of guilt and despair over her beloved only son made her boundlessly grateful for what she saw as Rasputin's curative powers. She gave Rasputin anything he wanted, and what Rasputin wanted was nothing less than to rule Imperial Russia. He convinced Alexandra to replace the liberal ministers to the court with weak men who allowed Rasputin to rule the country through them. His powers of clairvoyance were no help in ruling the country. The people were outraged. By 1915, most of the Duma and the liberal leaders around the country were conspiring to set up a more capable government and regain the faith of the people. A leader of the Duma and relatives of the Czar finally managed to get rid of Rasputin by assassination in 1916. But it was too late to restore confidence in the monarchy.

The war, like most wars, brought an increase in economic prosperity as factories and farms produced at full capacity to meet the needs of the military. Siberia supplied millions of *poods* of grain—a *pood* is 36.11 pounds—yearly. While inflation

Krasnoyarsk in 1914, a thriving city in Siberia.

began to eat away at the value of the money, a peasant family's wealth was measured by the number of their horses and the amount of land they farmed. Any peasant with property was called a *kulak.* Two or three horses and three to nine *dessiatins* of land made a *kulak* middle-class; four horses and ten or more *dessiatins* of land made him rich. Half the peasants in Siberia were rich by these standards. Many formed production and market cooperatives, or *artels,* and unions. The Union of Siberian Butter Artels, for instance, consisted of 563 artels and 502 artel shops. Credit artels provided for financial needs, and the peasants learned to manipulate credit and money.

But as the war dragged on the bubble broke. The military took the farm horses, taking away the peasants' wealth as well as their ability to farm. The military took the peasants, too, in increasing numbers and at all ages. Fifty percent of the male population went to war, and a large percentage never came back or returned with bitter stories of neglect and mismanagement in the field, of hunger and inadequate clothing for the cold. The war was going badly for the Russians, and defeat after defeat made the people lose all confidence in their leaders.

When, in February, 1917, disorders broke out in St. Petersburg, the leaders of the liberal groups in the Duma took advantage of the situation to urge Czar Nicholas II to abdicate. With surprising quickness, assured of safety, Nicholas agreed. This February Revolution brought about a peaceful transition to the "dual power" of a Provisional Government and the Soviets of Workers' and Soldiers' Deputies. The new Provisional Government was moderate. They left most of the bureaucratic processes in place, changing only the top-level people, thinking to effect gradual change. They presented plans to convene a Constituent Assembly to give Russia democratic representation in decision-making. They also decided that Russia's commitment to the Allies had to be honored; the war had to go on. The war cost money, so there could be no immediate appeasement of the people by redistribution of wealth. But rebellion was in the air. The Soviets of Workers' and Soldiers' Deputies objected violently to moderation and played on the impatience of the people: they had waited long enough; patience and moderation were not going to bring them what they wanted. The Provisional Government was eroded by this friction between the dual powers, leaving a hole for the Bolsheviks to move into. That small minority group grabbed the reins of power in the second revolution of 1917, the October Revolution.

Many books and papers have been written about how the Bolsheviks, together with the left-wing Social Democrats and Anarchists, managed this takeover. It was really the victory of one man, Vladimir Ilich Lenin, with his own idea of what the people should have and the determination to use any force, any terror, to achieve his ideas. Lenin wanted worldwide

Ekaterinburg, at the time Czar Nicholas II and the Russian royal family were assassinated in the cellar of a building.

communism, and saw the revolution in Russia as only the start of a wave of revolutions, each country falling one after the other like dominoes.

Lenin failed to convince the world to revolt, and he failed to achieve communism in Russia. His theory of communism was based on the philosophies of Karl Marx and Friedrich Engels: each person to give what he could and receive what he needed, the absence of class distinctions, the withering away of the state until governments were no longer needed as people handled their own affairs, the elimination of organized religion with its financial and emotional demands on its practitioners and its many divisive forms that caused persecution and wars, and the elimination of the family. Thus, every person would be socially, politically, and economically free and completely individual.

Lenin knew that communism could not be achieved immediately. Organized religion was abolished, and payments in kind rather than money were instituted. Property was seized from anyone who had it, including the peasants, and put into the hands of the government. But instead of "withering away," the government became more absolute. In fact, Lenin called his government a dictatorship, the Dictatorship of the Proletariat, the working class. The Dictatorship of the Proletariat was not even that; it was a dictatorship of Lenin and his followers, and they ruled by terror to achieve the subservience, not the independence, of the people. Power was in Lenin's hands, and he was determined to keep it by killing, imprisoning, or exiling dissidents, real or imaginary. This was Bolshevik Power, not the Power of the Proletariat. The soviets, the councils started in the Revolution of 1905, were supposed to be organs of communication between the people and their government, but they were used only to transmit the authority of government. It was armed authority, the authority of the Red Guards and the dreaded Cheka, forerunner of the KGB.

The new government ended the war with Germany, not only because the people were tired of war but also because the Germans paid the Bolsheviks to end it. The Germans had been paying the Bolsheviks from the time of the February Revolution to work toward ending the war. And it was the Germans who supplied Lenin with the train that brought him out of self-imposed exile into Russia to assume power in the October Revolution. The Germans were only too happy to bring the war with Russia to an end. With the Russian or Eastern Front closed, the Central Powers could concentrate all their forces against the Allies on the Western Front. Still Germany and Austro-Hungary forced a humiliating and harsh peace treaty on the Russians with the loss of much territory and the payment of severe reparations. This Treaty of Brest-Litovsk, signed in March, 1918, was declared null and void by Russia when World War I ended on November 11 of that year. This was probably anticipated by Lenin when he insisted that his negotiator, Leon Trotsky, sign the onerous treaty.

The royal family—Nicholas and Alexandra, the stricken Alexei, and his sisters—were taken to Ekaterinburg (now Sverdlovsk) in Western Siberia where they waited to be exiled to England. Instead, in 1918, they were shot to keep them from becoming the focus of a growing counterrevolutionary movement. If there was no royal family to reassume the throne, it was thought that the counterrevolution would sputter out and die. It did not.

Siberia, so far from the seat of power in the new Bolshevik capital of Moscow, so sparsely populated, saw little of the Revolution. But it was in Siberia that much of the counterrevolution took place. A civil war erupted, Reds or Bolsheviks against Whites or anti-Bolsheviks, and Siberia was the field of action. The fighting was brutal and bitter.

The abrupt ending of Russia's war with Germany added to the chaos of civil war in Siberia. Thousands of German prisoners held in Siberia had to be repatriated. And 70,000 Czechs, who had deserted the Germans to fight with the Russians, found themselves trapped. The Czechs only wanted to go home to Bohemia, as it was called then, but they would have to go through enemy German lines to get there. That didn't seem a good idea. It was decided instead that they would take the Trans-Siberian Railway across Siberia to Vladivostok and pick up Allied ships there to take them home via America or through the Indian Ocean and around Africa and north to Europe—or whatever way they could find. It could mean traveling around the world, a monumental journey. Just getting on the Railway meant weeks of waiting turns, so getting home might take months, possibly years.

The Czechs' epic trek had barely started when, at a station in Western Siberia, a fight broke out with German prisoners-of-war also on their way home—the quick way, straight to Germany. Red Guards, the Bolshevik militia, arrested some Czechs. This did not sit well with their companions, who promptly jumped off the train, disarmed the Reds, helped themselves to arms at the local ammunition depot, and took over the city. At the next stop, Red Guards were waiting to arrest them for this fracas, so they repeated the performance—and so on, down the line. Every day the Trans-Siberian train going east would bring more Czechs, 70,000 of them moving across Siberia, capturing town after town. They took Vladivostok at the end of the line even as the last Czechs were waiting to board the train in Europe. Everything in front of them having already been taken, these men captured two cities on the Volga River while they were waiting. With any kind of backup, they might have won the entire country. But they only wanted to go home and gave up their conquests in the same way a fisherman throws back a fish he doesn't want to eat but wants to catch just to show he can.

So here was Siberia, full of warring Czechs, Whites, and Reds. Then along came the British, the French, the Americans, and the Japanese. They came to Siberia to help Admiral Alexander Vasilyevich Kolchak, the leader of the Whites, in the hope that the Provisional Government could be restored. The Russians might then reopen the Eastern Front, badly needed to take pressure off the Western Front in France and Belgium while squeezing the Germans between them. The Allies were also anxious to keep the huge stockpiles of arms and ammunition they had sent the Russians out of the hands of the released German prisoners-of-war, who could carry a lot back to Germany. Each of the Allies had its individual concerns as well. The Americans were there to try to get the Czechs back into fighting World War I, not the Trans-Siberian War! And the Japanese, who had sent ten times as many men as all the others put together, were looking for an opportunity to grab Far Eastern Siberia.

Then it was November 11, 1918, and World War I was finally over. But the Allied troops stayed in Siberia, caught up in the fighting, trying to assist the refugees. Refugees were everywhere, displaced by the soldier-bandits roaming the countryside, stealing, burning, killing. Their atrocities would have put Tamerlane's to shame. The Allies wanted out, and offered to mediate between Reds and Whites. The Reds accepted the offer, but Admiral Kolchak refused. There can be no one-sided mediation, so the French, British, and Americans gave up trying and left Siberia. The Japanese stayed on and so did the French general Janin, who was appointed by the Allies to watch over the welfare of the Czechs.

The Czechs were still trying to get home. Reds and Whites wanted the Czechs to fight for them. Kolchak needed them desperately to replace his fast-deserting troops, and he ordered the tunnels of the Trans-Siberian Railway destroyed to stop the Czech trek across Siberia. General Janin was incensed. He was responsible for seeing that the Czechs got out, and see to it he would. He turned Admiral Kolchak over to the Reds. The leader of the Whites was put to death, and his treasury of a billion dollars or so in bullion and securities was taken by the Reds.

Into this chaos came a man from Chicago. Born in Russia, he had emigrated to the United States after a term or two in Siberia as a political prisoner. His name was Alexander Krasnoshchekov. In Chicago he worked as a tailor, attended the University of Chicago, and became a lawyer. Krasnoshcheckov, an ardent follower of Lenin, went back to Siberia when the Revolution broke out. In a short time he became the vice president of the first Workers' Conference in the Siberian Far East but was captured by the Whites and taken to Irkutsk for execution. Before sentence could be carried out, the Whites were themselves out of time, the war had more or less ended, and Krasnoshchekov found himself a Red, not a dead, hero.

He looked around, and what he saw were the Japanese, still in Siberia, still waiting their chance to take it. Krasnoshchekov knew that the country was too divided to defend itself against a Japanese takeover in the Siberian Far East. He also knew that almost any excuse would bring the Japanese into action. The establishment of a Bolshevik government would be an excellent excuse in the eyes of these capitalists. But a government was needed, or Siberia would be lost in anarchy and still ripe for Japanese plucking. Krasnoshchekov telephoned Lenin in Moscow (not an easy feat in those days) and outlined his plan: make Far Eastern Siberia, including Sakhalin Island, a separate country, but do not put Bolsheviks in charge. Japan would then have no excuse to intervene. Lenin agreed with the plan, and Krasnoshchekov drew up a Declaration of Independence for the new country. He wrote it in English, his more fluent language, and had it translated into Russian. And so, in 1920, the Independent and Democratic Far Eastern Republic was born.

The Japanese still did not leave. Nobody, including their former allies, knew what to do with them. But by 1922 the Reds had consolidated their positions and were clearly the rulers of Russia—or, as they named it, the Union of Soviet Socialist Republics. They sent the Red Army into the Inde-

Lenin seated at the head of the table around which crowd his Council of Ministers.

pendent and Democratic Far Eastern Republic, and took away its independence and democracy. Red troops moved toward Vladivostok, and in front of them fled thousands of White Russians who had taken refuge in the Republic. They left the country on every available kind of boat—and the Japanese went also. Its mission accomplished, the Far Eastern Republic was dissolved.

Siberia settled in to learn how to live with what was then called the Communist Party (Bolsheviks). It was not easy. All industry, trade, and agriculture was nationalized, run by the government. Wages were not paid in money but in kind—in vouchers for food, transportation, and housing. The prosperous individual farms of Siberia were turned into collectives called *kolkhozes.* Many peasants, reminded of the days of serfdom, refused to join the *kolkhozes* and were hauled off to prison camps. The *kolkhozes* produced poorly. The suddenly impoverished and bewildered people were forced to labor for some government they didn't know or care about and to give their labors for next-to-nothing. Compulsory food deliveries had to be made to cities and government officials, even though the deliverers starved. So-called Committees of the Poor, made up of peasants, laborers, and often criminals, confiscated food and property and went wild with their new-found power. The *kulaks* lost their farms and other property and were deprived of all rights, in an attempt to wipe them out as a class. The term "*kulak*" was applied very loosely; even the poorest person who incurred someone's dislike could be shunted off to Siberia as a *kulak.* There were many uprisings and strikes, and five million peasant households were to drop out of sight, sent to remote Siberian settlements or to the corrective labor camps that were organized in 1918 at the direction of Lenin. Communism, the equal sharing of all goods and property, was not equalizing, was not working or workable.

Lenin realized that he needed to strengthen the political base of his Communist Party (Bolsheviks) by first restoring the economy. He came up with the N.E.P.—the New Economic Policy. Private enterprise and the use of money was allowed on a limited basis in agriculture, industry, and trade. It worked, and protests died down. But at the same time those who ran these private enterprises, the "N.E.P. men," or "Nepmen," were badly discriminated against socially, politically, and in the courts. Even their children faced discrimination, and were not admitted to good schools. And when the N.E.P. was ended in 1927, the Nepmen were ended too, their property confiscated, they and their families sent to Siberian forced-labor camps. Yet these men had acted at Lenin's direction and had helped consolidate the power of the Communists.

But there were more and worse injustices to come under the dictatorship, not of the proletariat, but of one man, Josef Stalin, successor to Lenin. Stalin was to finally fill the vast spaces of Siberia, fill them with millions of victims of his power—and mania.

7

The Prisoners of Siberia

W E DO NOT KNOW what life was like for the early
prisoners of Siberia. They left no records, no written
accounts or letters; they are as silent as the tongue-
less bell of Uglich. So the story of the prisoners of Siberia does
not begin until 1825, with a revolt that captured the imaginations
of people around the world, the first Russian Revolution.

Many well-educated Russian aristocrats in the early 1800s
deplored serfdom and poverty in their country. A few of these
men, of high military rank and members of royal court circles,
somehow came to believe that a more enlightened, liberal
leadership should result if they assassinated the new czar-to-
be, Nicholas I. They attempted a poorly planned assassination
on the occasion of his coronation in December, 1825, and were
quickly caught. Five were hung, and the rest sent to Siberia.
They were young, fabulously wealthy, highly privileged—and
they had thrown it all away to help the poor peasants of Russia.

Czar Nicholas I, whom the Decembrists attempted to assassinate on the day of his inauguration.

Naturally, they became heroes. They were dubbed the De-cembrists, or Dekabrists, after the date of their rather pitiful revolt.

Far more heroic than the men were the wives who voluntarily followed the exiles into Siberia. These women were innocent of any plotting, of any attempt at murder. A number were young pampered princesses and countesses from families of great wealth and power. They could have remarried, because exile brought automatic dissolution of marriage. Instead, they chose to follow their husbands, leaving babies behind, traveling across Siberia for months, to live under primitive conditions with no rights at all and at the mercy of their husbands' jailers.

Their letters and diaries give us some idea of life in the prison system of Siberia, although the Decembrists were not your everyday kind of exiles. Most were fortunate enough to still have a great deal of money of their own. They were able to build homes, and in fact the Decembrists were responsible for the building and development of one of Siberia's major cities, Chita. They had pianos and art materials and books and other comforts sent to them by their families and soon learned how to make the most of their situation, although the climate and sometimes brutal jailers and poor medical care killed some whose health was fragile.

Political exiles were treated far better than criminal exiles, and, Russia being an aristocracy, the higher-ranking exiles were treated best of all, whether they were political or criminal. The Decembrists usually had their own rooms, sometimes more than one, in the prison camps. They could furnish the rooms as they pleased, with rugs and drapes and pictures and books. Working in the mines or felling trees was hard for these aristocrats, but they did not spend much time at it, as other prisoners did. And their wives could visit freely, leaving only at night for their own comfortable quarters.

Other political exiles—and there were many, particularly in the last quarter of the nineteenth century—did not fare so well as the Decembrists. They brought no wives or husbands to make life easier for them, although some pretended to be engaged to be married because engaged couples were allowed to visit one another. Some did marry. Lenin himself married during a three-year term of imprisonment in Siberia. Most of these political exiles, referred to simply as "politicals," were men and women between the ages of eighteen and twenty-eight. They were firebrands, hard to manage, quick to rebel, and with a good deal of snobbery in them despite their fighting for equality. On the whole, they were not mistreated, although the books and letters they wrote indicate that they were highly indignant most of the time at anything less than perfect courtesy from guards and prison officials.

After the building of the Trans-Siberian Railway, politicals made the first part of the journey by train, joining convoys of prisoners in Siberia. The convoys were like freight trains, perhaps a mile or so long, moving slowly down the Moscow Track, their chains clanking in a peculiar cadence recognized from miles away. The older men, men who were not first-time offenders and therefore wise in the ways of the road, walked in front, relatively free from the dust or spattering of mud kicked up by the convoy. Then came the rest of the convicts with free wives or husbands and children accompanying them. Behind them were the two-wheeled carts for baggage, on top of which the sick, the exhausted, and a few children could ride. And bringing up the rear were the politicals, a guard for each, making up a kind of caboose.

The human freight moved from 16 to 20 miles a day, resting every third day. This was a journey that could last two years, a journey so hard that the government provided for new shoes to be issued periodically to everyone, including the free companions of the convicts. The Moscow Track was a misery of dust in dry weather and a sea of mud in wet. In winter the prisoners froze. In summer they were driven mad by the dreaded Siberian midges and mosquitoes, unless they had been knowledgeable enough to provide themselves with horsehair nets to drape over their heads. When they reached the rivers they were loaded onto barges, sometimes so carelessly that the barges sank and many of them drowned, dragged down by fetters or clothing. When the rivers were frozen the convoys plodded along on the ice or waited over the winter in

Prisoner convoy walking across Siberia.

Prison buildings were usually next to a church.

prison cells, something the politicals dreaded and fought to avoid. They preferred getting to their places of detention, usually wooden barracks with yards where they would have more freedom and companionship than in the transit cells.

On the road, free wives and husbands were thrown together with convicts in one hodge-podge mass and treated in much the same way. Politicals kept themselves separate, the men gallantly watching out for the welfare of the women and screening off sleeping areas for them. But everyone else slept side-by-side on the bare, sloping ledge that served as one huge bed, women and children mixed with criminals of the lowest kind. Often the convoy stations—*etappuy*—were filthy, stoves unworkable, the walls covered with beetles and roaches. People were not free of insects either, or of the diseases they caused.

The prison camps were not much better than the convoy stations as far as sanitation was concerned, and some were worse. When Sakhalin was turned into a prison island there were no latrines or rubbish pits for years. Well water and the ground was a mess of garbage and human excrement. Kara Prison did not have a latrine or ditch or even a pail for toileting purposes until 1878. Prisoners were simply let out into a courtyard at one fixed time to relieve themselves, much like dogs. Naturally, epidemics raged, often out of control because of the shortage of medical help and medicines. Other prisons had more sensible and sanitary arrangements, including bath-houses the prisoners were made to use at least weekly. Politicals made it a point of pride to keep their rooms and their persons clean and neat, but many convicts were not interested in personal hygiene and lived in indescribable filth.

There were only a few kinds of Siberian sentences for politicals and criminals: solitary confinement in the isolator (a building with individual cells) at Irkutsk, usually for the most

Prisoners squeezed together on bare sloping boards or ledges that served as beds. Double-decked and head-to-head in most prisons, bed ledges remain part of Siberian prison life.

violent of the politicals; hard labor, (*katorga*), for a fixed number of years followed by a term of supervised settlement, for both politicals and convicts; detention without hard labor, for politicals and usually for three years and often but not always followed by settlement; and settlement without detention, usually reserved for whole groups of peasants moved from their villages for some disobedience or another, perhaps even imaginary ones. The key word was "settlement," for Russia wanted these exiles to hold and develop Siberia. Unfortunately, most prisoners were kept in detention so long that by the time they reached settler status they were too worn out, too old, and too poorly motivated to contribute to the building of a country.

Hard labor could mean many things. Often hard labor

Women convicts drawing a water cart.

wasn't very hard, particularly for politicals. Politicals and the better-educated convicts worked in offices or used skills they had used when they were free, like barbering or blacksmithing. Really hard labor might be on the Trans-Siberian Railway or in the mines and was the convicts' lot. It is possible that some politicals were quietly disposed of by assignments to these places. Life sentences to hard labor didn't last too long in some of the mines; a couple of years or so and the prisoner was dead. There were many kinds of mines, particularly as construction of the Railway turned up many important minerals. The salt mines were harder to work than the gold mines, for instance. Prisoners were not always unhappy about being assigned to gold mines. The gold had a way of sticking to some hands—and much of it found its way into the pockets of the prison authorities. All the gold was the private, personal property of the Czar, and stealing it was a personal offense against his person. In other words, it was dangerous to get caught. Most didn't. But when supplies dwindled suspiciously, convicts—and prison authorities—were replaced by free and hopefully honest laborers who were expected not to steal because they were paid wages.

Private companies ran the other mines, the government providing prisoner labor, food, coal for heat, construction materials, transportation, and so forth, in return for rents. Lumbering operations were run the same way. Prisoners were used for cutting down the trees and then chained to the logs to haul them out of the *taiga*. Carpenters, too, had to chain-haul the lumber they needed for their projects.

Prisoners were also used as house servants and were virtually slaves. Free men and women could have been used for the jobs, but they would have had to be paid full wages. Prisoners were paid 10 percent of customary wages, only half of which was given to them at the time. The other half was held until they were released. If they died before that time, the money was paid to their heirs—if officials bothered to look for them.

Prisoners with money could escape their hard labor sentences completely by paying convicts to work for them. But sentences of hard labor resulted in a loss of family and property rights, and of class—and classless people had no papers or internal passports allowing them freedom of movement. Only after ten years as a settler could some exiles get permission to enroll in the peasant class. As a peasant with an internal passport an exile could travel, although only in Siberia, and could find a job. Some could even manage to escape Siberia,

A young political prisoner seems proud to demonstrate his shackles in this studio photograph. Diamond-shaped patches on the long overcoats or shubas indicated by color whether the wearer was a political or a convict.

if they had enough money and connections. Some were able to get to America if they were in Far Eastern Siberia and able to get aboard a ship crossing the Pacific. But many did not have the means or the drive to leave, or had nothing to go back to, and they stayed on in Siberia even after their exile status had ended and they were completely free.

Life in Siberia depended not only on the sentence but also on the places to which prisoners were sent. The farther north and east or the smaller the settlement, the more difficult the journey to it and the harder the life. In many places, particularly above the Arctic Circle, there might be only two or three tiny settlements of a few huts in a radius of perhaps 2,000 miles. Not only was the isolation hard, but the climate was harsher, the dark winters longer. And comforts like tea, sugar, lamp oil, and even that staple of the Russian diet, bread, were often not available, because it was so hard to get supplies to these remote areas.

Politicals could earn their freedom by renouncing their beliefs, but only a very few did so. Their beliefs were too strong. Their beliefs were also varied. Some were activists who believed in provoking the guards and administrators, others wanted no part of any actions that would bring further punishments down on their heads. Some politicals were not really political at all. They might have been friends of a political or caught up in a general sweep of suspects and sent to Siberia by administrative exile rather than trial. But they all organized into communal groups—artels—in the face of authority.

While convict artels were dominated by the strongest man, a gangster chieftain who had the power of life and death over his fellow prisoners, political artels were democratic. Each man who joined (it was not compulsory) had an equal vote, and the majority ruled. Disputes were settled by the artel, chores were assigned, food bought, and finances handled. Money came from home, from government allowances for food and labor, and from sales of small items like cigarettes and boxes made by the prisoners. Actual money was never given to the prisoners; all transactions were on paper. The artel pooled the men's credits, buying extra meat or tobacco or candles or delicacies for the ill or a holiday feast. The daily ration per person around the turn of the century was 6 ounces of meat, a few ounces of meal for soup or cereal, some salt, and 3¼ pounds of bread. There was nothing in that diet to prevent scurvy, and many prisoners suffered great pain and loss of teeth and bone breakage from that disease. Pooling their money might mean the purchase of a precious—expensive—fruit or vegetable to help restore health.

Politicals were not allowed to write letters until they achieved settler status. Letters and gifts from relatives and friends were relayed through the commandant, who could conceivably keep them. Fortunately this did not happen often. Although some prison officials were thieves, they preferred to steal big. It was easy, for instance, to keep the names of dead men on the prisoner rosters and receive government payments for their supposed labor and meals.

Political prisoners, unafraid of punishment, often staged strikes or made demands for better bread or more lamps or longer exercise periods or whatever. Usually they won their points, but not always. At Yakutsk in 1889, a group of young politicals on their way north to the Kolyma Prison protested that the way they were to be transported was unnecessarily hard. They were told to go to the police office with their complaints, but sure that nothing good awaited them there, they refused to move. Infuriated guards clubbed and bayonet-ted and shot them. Six were killed, including pregnant women,

Convicts had their hair shaved off on one side of the head only, as a means of identification.

and 27 were wounded. A stupid commandant had three more
executed and sentenced 19 to life imprisonment, but public
indignation at the unwarranted brutality ran so high that they
were granted amnesty. However, in the next year the government hardened its position on politicals. Trials were suspended
and prisoners sent to Siberia by administrative exile instead.
And prison officials were instructed to grant politicals fewer
courtesies and concessions.

Loneliness and despair led to a number of suicides among
politicals, but they were not physically mistreated as convicts
were. After the Great Reforms of Czar Alexander II in the
1860s, convicts could no longer be beaten to death or rolled in
barrels until they died. But the penal code allowed punishment
without any investigation. Convicts could still be flogged—and
die "accidentally"—for not taking their hats off quickly enough
when addressed by a guard or for dozens of other petty
reasons. In Voyevodsk Prison, considered the worst, convicts
had to drag heavy iron balls and chains as they worked. In the
mines, a convict could be chained to his wheelbarrow twenty-
four hours a day, never leaving it, often for terms of a year or
more.

The lives of the convicts were quite different from that of
the politicals. Convicts were of all kinds—intelligent and sub-
human, embezzlers and petty thieves, rapists and murderers,
and, too often, innocent victims of the policy of administrative
exile without trial, often victims of someone's hatred or anti-
Semitism or other prejudices. Anti-Semitism, including po-
groms—violent raids by Cossacks on Jewish villages—was
rampant in Russia under the czars. Jews did not have the civil
rights of other Russian citizens and were discriminated against
even in exile. Husbands could not follow wives into Siberia,
and while wives could follow husbands, children had to be

Yard of Kara Prison for political prisoners around 1900.

left behind unless they were being nursed. That kept most Jewish wives at home. Wives at home, whatever their religion, received some government support, but never enough. Although they might have been heartbroken, the wives who stayed at home were far better off then those who went with their husbands.

Officials were supposed to look out for the welfare of free wives who followed husbands, but few did. In some Siberian prisons, free wives were kept in wards just like the convicts. And free women had much harder lives than women convicts. The convicts usually had their sentences reduced and were released from detention in a short time, given a house, and issued prison rations for two years. As women were very scarce in Siberia, men settlers came from far and near to look the women over on the day of release. A few minutes to exchange names, and the woman might sign herself over to the man as a laborer and leave with him. A woman without a man to protect her was faced with so many dangers and problems that prisoners would forego their own houses to move in with any man. Marriage was usually the next step, after a one- to three-year period of what was called "cohabitation." Sometimes the commandment decided which settlers could get a woman, so buying the privilege was a fairly common practice. The men didn't mind the money. They got it back in free services. And, if a man married for the first time, his wife would be given 15 roubles by the government as a wedding gift that the groom could pocket. Free women had to rent houses and were unable to arrange protective marriages unless their husbands consented to divorce, in which case the women received 50 roubles on remarrying. Since the women had come to Siberia only out of loyalty to their husbands, they usually did not divorce. But their husbands were held in detention for years, and eventually almost all the "free" wives had to resort to prostitution to support themselves and their children.

Children had an equally dreary fate. There were many children. In Sakhalin children under fifteen made up one-fourth of the population. Although there were churches, there were no schools, and the only education a child might get was an occasional hour or two of tutoring by the more-educated prisoners. In many families, girl children were valuable commodities to be sold into marriage when they reached fourteen or fifteen, fetching prices that were often high enough to make parents comfortable for life. Food rations were provided by the government for the very young children, but mothers also had to eat. The government also gave allowances to the poorest families, but there were many different interpretations of who was "poorest." Families lived on nothing but turnips for months, and death from malnutrition was common. Most children turned beggar.

There were many beggar-prisoners in Siberia. Prisoners were allowed to leave their barracks, and those in need would approach a house or shop or travelers along the road, and sing mournful, pleading little begging songs. People would give them a few kopecks (pennies) or a bit of bread. (Small pieces of bread were used as money throughout Siberia.) These men were the weakest of the criminals, and the most defenseless. The proceeds from their begging were often stolen and, unless they were very careful, so was their clothing.

Clothing was a valuable commodity in Siberia, and considered worth stealing. Every two years the men prisoners were issued new gray trousers and long gray overblouses and belts, and each winter men and women convicts were given new *shubas*—long felt overcoats, very heavy and warm. The soldiers who guarded the convicts did not get reissues of clothing that frequently, and settlers did not get any. The result was a brisk black market in prisoners' used clothing, sometimes run by prison officials. The guards might steal the clothing and then flog the prisoners for having "lost" or "gambled away" state property. Losing one's clothing in a card game was not unusual. Card playing was a mania in Siberia, and clothes were valuable stakes.

Murder was commonplace and fear ruled them all. Settlers, often former prisoners themselves or descendants of prisoners, would kill prisoner-beggars for their clothes or out of fear of being killed themselves. And beggars would kill settlers for a loaf of bread or out of fear or hatred or for no reason at all.

Most feared were the tramps, convicts who were trying to make their escape. They were rarely hunted—they weren't

Childen of convict laborers on the Trans-Siberian Railway.

worth the trouble—and could easily evade recapture. But most had no place to go and simply wandered through Siberia. People rarely refused to feed them. Indeed, many peasants left food out at all times for any tramps who might come along, hoping to avoid having their homes invaded by vengeful thieves and murderers. But the peasants also formed secret hunting parties to kill tramps and collect the rewards the government had on their heads. Peasants had other tricks as well. They would hire tramps to help them, often for months at a time, then pay them off, kill them somewhere down the road, repocket the wages they had paid out, and claim the government reward for "capturing" a runaway prisoner.

A captured prisoner was resentenced and would rarely leave detention. But the other prisoners, convict and political, would find their sentences shortened somewhat by the Russian Penal Code and imperial edicts could shorten them further. The usual ten-year sentence ran about eight years, life sentences about twenty years. One way or another, eventually all detention came to an end, and prisoners became settlers under supervision. There were no differences between forced settlers and free, except that poor discharge planning often sent forced settlers to overcrowded villages without enough farmland or homesteads, so that they had to double up, while single men were sent to underdeveloped areas badly needing whole families. Settlements failed, and settlers failed, unable to farm or otherwise support themselves except by loans at high rates of interest from wealthy convicts and peasants, loans they had a hard time repaying.

Politicals usually fared better. Many were educated and had skills that were needed in the developing cities and towns of Siberia. A political prisoner in the Amur region conducted the first census, traveling from town to town as an honored government official. Some families were able to send money, and the politicals could set up in businesses and professions.

Then the Revolution of 1917 freed the political prisoners of Siberia. They had won their cause against despotism—or so they thought.

8

The Prisoners of Stalin

THE MEN WHO grabbed power in the October Revolution were a small minority group whose ideas clashed with those of many other revolutionaries. But Lenin and his cohorts were far better organized than the other groups, and more ruthless. They rid themselves of their opponents through the effective use of terror, administered by what they termed security organs: first the Red Guards and the Cheka, then the GPU, MGB, MVD, NKGB, NKVD, and since 1953 the KGB—the Russian abbreviation for "Committee of State Security." Whatever their names, they were essentially the same instruments of control. And they quickly filled the prison camps and graves of Siberia.

In the aftermath of the October Revolution, politicals who did not come over to the Bolsheviks were executed or forced to flee the country—or found themselves in Siberia once again. Later, even staunch Bolsheviks were to join them in exile. And political exile under the Communist Party (Bolsheviks) was immeasurably worse than under the czars.

Lenin had been exiled to Siberia from 1897 to 1900. He was able to write and study and get married. Stalin had been banished six times, once to an Arctic settlement of only three huts. He had escaped five times, but only the revolution ended his sixth sentence. One would think that these former prisoners would have put an end to the prisons camps of Siberia. Instead, they turned Siberia into a huge slave labor and death camp, passing the formula on to Hitler for his concentration camps. The first Siberian "corrective labor camps," as they were called, were organized in 1918. In 1920, the milder "corrective labor colonies" were built near Siberian industrial areas to supply workers from among prisoners serving minor, usually three-year, sentences.

The slightest hint of dissent, even the possibility of dissent, was choked off by these former dissenters. They knew how they had toppled one of the most powerful monarchies in the world, and they were not going to allow the same thing to happen to them. Three-man tribunals, called *troikas,* meaning threesome, like the three-horse carriages and sleighs, were set up all over the country to expedite the removal of people to Siberian prison camps and colonies without trial. Thousands of peasants, many of whom had supported the Reds, were imprisoned because they refused to give the land they had only just won from the czars to enter the *kolkhozes,* the farm collectives. Citizens were encouraged to spy on one another and curried favor by reporting the smallest, most offhand criticism of the new regime. Friends and relatives were afraid to talk to one another or to neighbors. Each dwelling had a woman installed as a kind of concierge or doorlady to report on the comings and goings of all the tenants. Children were encouraged to spy on parents. One fourteen-year-old who turned in his parents to die in Siberia was killed by relatives in revenge and is memorialized as a martyr in the Soviet Union.

In the first few years of communism, under Lenin, conditions in the Siberian camps remained fairly civilized. As they had been under the czars, prisoners were reasonably well fed and clothed. They worked only six hours a day in winter, ten in summer. But conditions soon worsened. Discontent was growing in the land. The socialist nonmoneyed society was not working. The food supply was failing; the *kolkhozes* weren't producing as well as the individual farms had. Not only was the cooperative system not working, but thousands of farm workers had been put in Siberian prison camps. The *kulaks* were eliminated almost to a man, and anybody who didn't like someone simply had to accuse him of being a *kulak* to be rid of him. Hunger and discontent bred criticism, and critics swelled the population of the camps to overflowing.

New camps were set up, most in the north and east, far from the Trans-Siberian Railway. There were so many prisoners being sent into Siberia that winter stopovers were no longer possible as they had been in the days of the czars. Convoys had to struggle through blowing and deep snow and icy winds in temperatures going down to $-60°$ and $-70°$ F. Prisoners died as they walked, or were shot if they lagged. One convoy of several thousand prisoners with guards lost its way, and every last person died.

Snowstorms in the winter of 1932–1933 were blamed for preventing food from reaching camps, so that thousands of prisoners died of starvation. The supplies were probably never sent, because by this time a deliberate plan to kill as many prisoners as possible was becoming evident. Thousands were also dying of hunger outside the camps. Many observers and historians claim that the great famine of this time was artificial, deliberately engineered to exacerbate the effects of a drought and underproduction by peasants who would not produce without making a profit of some kind. The idea was to force the peasants to submit to collectivization, particularly in the fertile Ukraine, where famine reached unprecedented proportions, leading to incidents of cannibalism.

Josef Vissarionovich Stalin had maneuvered into power as the leader of the Soviet Union after Lenin's death in 1924. Lenin was revered; his mummified body lay in a glass coffin in the Kremlin as in a shrine, people constantly filing by in silent homage. (They still do.) Stalin wanted this same godlike status, this reverence and total obedience to him as absolutely and personally all-powerful. This demand for personal worship disturbed the members of the Central Committee, who were the ostensible ruling body of the country with Stalin as their head. One Committee member, Sergey Mironovich Kirov, who had been a close friend and strong supporter of Stalin, is believed to have led the opposition to Stalin's personality cult. In December of 1934, Kirov was shot and killed, probably at Stalin's orders, although he expressed great outrage and used the shooting as an excuse to start a purge of his opponents, real and imaginary, that was to turn Siberia into a hell.

The Great Purge, called in the Soviet Union the *"yezhovsh-china"* after Nikolai Yezhov, then the head of the NKVD and a depraved sadist, is considered the bloodiest time in all of Russia's bloody history. The Purge eliminated almost all the Central Committee—including staunch Stalinists fallen from grace—and the Politburo, the chief policy-making bureau, and all high-ranking military officers. The Purge reached across boundaries and oceans in assassinations of those who thought to escape Stalin's reach. Leon Trotsky, Lenin's great supporter,

The dreaded Yezhov

leader of the Petrograd Soviet that had accomplished the October Revolution, and negotiator of the Brest-Litovsk Treaty of 1917, had already been deprived of all power and expelled from the world Communist Party and the Soviet Union by Stalin when he was denounced in the Great Purge as a spy and subversive. He was living in Mexico City when he was assassinated in 1940, undoubtedly by Soviet agents, although this was never legally proved.

By the middle of 1936, arrests in the Great Purge were almost indiscriminate. Jews, Muslims, and many others who lived by religious tenets, forbidden by the Communists, suffered greatly. So did members of minority nationalities. Since everyone but the Great Russians were considered minority nationalities, prejudices ran rampant. The *troikas* were busy handing out sentences of death by shooting or imprisonment in Siberia on charges of treason or espionage or conspiracy or sabotage, the only evidence being confessions to anything the authorities wanted, confessions obtained by torture or threat of harm to loved ones. There was no right to appeal, and when sentences were over they were almost always extended without explanation. Ten years became twenty, and twenty became forever.

A few public trials were held, but they were merely show trials to impress the public with the injustices being done to their long-suffering leader and father-figure, Stalin. This image of Stalin was only one of a long series of myths and fictions told by Soviet authorities to this day as a kind of public relations ploy. Experts on the Soviet Union characterize "fictions" as more or less temporary, for outsider consumption. "Myths" are more pervasive, deeply imbedded beliefs that the Soviets themselves are meant to hold. A member of an early study group for the dissemination of such myths and fictions told of how he responded to a question with the name of the leader of a particular skirmish in the October Revolution. He himself had fought beside the man, so the answer came easily. But the man he named had since been declared an Enemy of the People, and therefore could not be a hero of the Revolution, could not have led the skirmish. The bewildered study group member asked how he could name anyone else as the leader— and found himself arrested that very night and sent off to Siberia for many long years. He, too, had become one of the Enemies of the People.

Stalin justified his Great Purge as an "inevitable class struggle on the road to full socialism." Actually, he had long given up the idea of full socialism, which required worldwide revolution. He wouldn't tell his people that; the myth of full socialism had to be maintained, unlike the lesser fictions that were changeable. What could he say? That he was killing some 10,000,000 people in order to insure his absolute power over the country? But that is what he did and what the Purge was about, and Stalin did achieve his goal.

The Great Purge more or less ended in 1938, and the sadistic Yezhov was disposed of in some unknown way by his successor as head of the Soviet security organs, Lavrentiy Pavlovich Beria. Beria was an equally sinister figure. The Great Purge may have ended, but Beria started his own reign of terror. A factory worker who took a day or two off without permission, the reader of an unauthorized book, the person who complained a bit about having to stand in line for hours to buy a bar of soap that didn't lather—off they went to the corrective labor camps, most never to be heard from again. Innocent wives were sent to Siberia, not as voluntary companions to husbands, as in the days of the czars, but as prisoners, as counterrevolutionists and Enemies of the People, on the theory that they must have shared in whatever their husbands were accused of. Husbands and wives were not sent to the same labor camps, and children were left behind, some to die of starvation and neglect. Millions of families were destroyed.

Stalin's labor camps and colonies were administered by the *Gulag.* "Gulag" is an abbreviation for the Russian words for "Chief Administration of Camps." Northern Siberia became known as the "Gulag Archipelago" when the novel by that name written by Alexander Solzhenitsyn, a former prisoner, was published in the West. That novel, and his *A Day in the Life of Ivan Denisovich,* published in 1962, made the Western world aware of the horrors of the Siberian camps. A few much earlier eye-witness accounts were published in the West by escapees or were smuggled out by the *samizdat* (meaning "self-publishing"), the underground network circulating unauthorized writings. But these reports had more or less escaped notice or were not fully believed in the West. Ironically, it took a work of fiction to make the truth known.

In northeast Siberia, in the Kolyma area rich in gold and tarnished by some of the worst of the camps, a subdivision of the Gulag called the "Dalstroy" was in charge. The heads of Dalstroy were almost as unlucky as the slave laborers under them. No matter how ruthless they were, they could not extract blood from the stones nor more gold from their slave laborers. No matter how honest they were, their superiors in Moscow decided they were holding back, that there must be more gold than they were getting. Some were, some weren't, but they all found their jobs very short-term and unrewarding. One after another of these all-powerful heads of Dalstroy was shot or disappeared, his wife sent to a labor camp. It could not have been a job one took voluntarily, although having reached the height of power, each must have thought he would be the one to survive.

Dalstroy and the Gulag were responsible not only for administering the camps but also for the work they produced. All of the construction in Siberia to about 1960 and probably later—the roads, the second tracks and new lines of the Trans-Siberian Railway, the power stations, the dams, the factories—was done by the prisoner labor. All kinds of industries, fishing camps, and farms bought prisoners. They drew up formal agreements stating costs and provisions for return, and so forth, all very businesslike—but the product being negotiated was a human being. Not that the human beings minded. Being bought often meant improved living conditions, since businesses tend to value their various properties and care for them, living or inanimate.

All sentences to Siberia were for hard labor. Families at home trying to find out their loved one's sentence lined up at special booths set up for the purpose. They quickly learned that a sentence to "hard labor for ten years without communication privileges" was really a sentence of execution already carried out.

But amidst all the death sentences and the killing in camps, where you could be put to death for not fulfilling a norm (production quota) that was impossible to fill, there was no death penalty for criminals until 1953: in Siberia under the Soviets the criminals, not the politicals, were the privileged prisoners. Norms were set from the time of Stalin's first Five-Year Plan for the economic development of the country in 1928. The Five-Year Plans broke down into exact numbers the amount of production expected from every farm, every factory, and every corrective labor camp and colony. Norms were always set far higher than was realistic. If anyone pointed out that the norms could not be met without other conditions being met—like enough boats to bring in the projected number of fish, or even enough fish in the waters—he or she was branded counterproductive and sentenced to Siberia. In the camps if daily norms were not met, food was taken away in the same percentages—20 percent below norm meant 20 percent less food next day. Less food meant weaker laborers, who then produced even less. This could go on until the workers starved to death or were shot for counterproductivity.

The women suffered most in the camps and on the nightmarish transit ships used to bring prisoners into the northeastern camps from Vladivostok. They did not have the physical strength to protect themselves or their belongings.

Many were victims of gang rape by convicts, who passed on multiple venereal diseases and caused pregnancies. Pregnancies were particularly hard, emotionally and physically. Many babies were born dead, and those that lived were taken away to be reared in nurseries. For the first few weeks mothers were allowed to feed their infants after the work of the day had been completed. After that, the mothers could see their children only once a month for two hours. In the peak work months of May through September even two hours a month was considered too long to be away from their work, and visits were suspended. Most children did not know their mothers from visit to visit. But even though they were not remembered, or the result of rape, the children were usually cherished by their prisoner mothers, who had nothing and nobody else. Then, sometime between the ages of two and seven, the children were taken away and put into a state home. By government regulation, mother and child would never see one another again.

Most women were sent to lumbering, farming, or fishing camps, considered easier than the mines. Farming was. But at the fishing camps on the islands and shores of the Arctic Ocean, the labor was more difficult. A two-person team had to gut 1,700 salmon or pack and salt 6,600 salmon a day, and each of those salmon had to be dug out of huge vats. The continuous bending and stretching, the pain of brine and salt getting into the many scrapes and cuts on the women's arms was agony. Sawing down trees and splitting logs was as bad. Only when the temperature was $-50°$ F. or below were the women permitted to stay in camp. Arguments about the temperature, which guards often misread in order to make sure that norms were filled, were understandably bitter and usually lost.

Women seemed to survive better than the men, however. Those few women who, like Eugenia Guinsberg, were able to write about the camps, felt that women endured better because they were more used to pain. Women could also get camp jobs as nurses or get extra bread or warm clothes by prostituting themselves.

Conditions varied in different camps. None were good, but some were worse than others. The tin mines were not too terrible but the lead mines eventually killed everyone by lead poisoning. Uranium mines killed with radioactivity and coal mines killed with coal dust in the lungs. Gypsum dust killed like coal dust, but gypsum mining was considered worse because of the particular harshness and size of the gypsum crystals that lodged in the lungs.

Each camp seemed to have a worse one to which prisoners could be sent as punishment. They might be punished for not fulfilling their norms, or for being unable to leave their beds one morning. Any attempts to reason with a guard, or a defensive lifting of the hand when hit or threatened, was considered an act of violence, punishable by death. Entire work groups, called "brigades," were sentenced to death if a few old or sick members could not contribute and the others could not cover up for them. The end of the line was a camp like the Serpantinka, where men were killed by the carbon monoxide poisoning in backs of trucks, or were shot. Waiting to die, they were packed so tightly into the rooms of the prison that they could not reach for the drinking water offered them but had to catch it in their mouths. It took a little longer to die at the infamous Unit 8 in the Shturmovoy mine, where conditions were so bad that no one survived more than a month.

Living tents were open to the cold, beds had no blankets

or mattresses to crawl under, and there were no lamps for the twenty-hour winter nights. As punishment, men and women might be made to stand naked all night long in temperatures of −60° F., or in summer the mosquito nets were taken away, and prisoners had no protection against the insects that bit or burrowed under their skin. The Siberian midges and mosquitoes are so vicious and numerous that they have been known to drive thick-skinned cattle so mad they galloped to their deaths.

The prisoners called themselves *katorzhniki*, from the old czarist term for hard labor, *katorga*. But this *katorga* was far worse than anything the czars had come up with. In some camps no one—not one single person—survived, ever, in the forty or so years the camps operated. It is difficult—impossible—to understand the thinking that went into creating this Siberia. There can be no understanding the moral wrong, but even considered as a way to create a cheap labor supply, why deliberately kill that supply off? Were there so many people that, like paper towels, it was cheaper to throw them away than to care for them so that they could be reused? Or was it to intimidate the population at large, or to focus their attention on something other than the difficult conditions communism had brought them, as Hitler focused all blame for everything on the Jews, so that he and his decisions would seem faultless? Whatever the reasons, sane people will never understand them. There can be no understanding of how a few madmen could kill so many millions of people and ruin the lives of hundreds of millions more, to turn our twentieth century, a time of great technical advances, into the darkest time in all human history.

9

The Great Patriotic War

LTHOUGH IT hardly seems possible, life in Siberia was to get worse as World War II raged. The Soviet Union did not enter the war in Europe until 1941 and used her Siberian slaves to increase her military and industrial strength during the two years of her nonintervention pact with Germany. Industries in the European section of the Soviet Union that were vulnerable to attack were moved into Siberia. Siberia was out of bombing range, and no invading army would venture into its vastness; they could not maintain supply lines or tolerate the terrain or weather. And Siberian prison camps and colonies offered an endless supply of labor.

The labor supply was so enlarged by arriving prisoners that rations were cut in half to accommodate them all, and the already overlong working day was increased. Not fulfilling a norm was considered sabotage. Camp commanders tried to outdo one another in their shows of patriotism, committing their camps to impossibly difficult tasks that caused thousands more deaths. Prisoners were shot at random to increase terror and force harder or faster or longer periods of work.

Stalin and Hitler had allied their two countries with the Nazi-Soviet Pact, two treaties signed in August and September, 1939, just as the Germans marched into Poland to start the war. The land grab was on. In October, 1939, with Hitler's permission, the Soviets took a piece of Poland it had given to Poland in 1920 and re-annexed it to Belorussia. Four and one-half million Poles went along with the territory, and many were turned into Siberian slave laborers as Stalin's growing demand for Russianization resulted in the oppression of all other peoples. In 1940, the Soviets took three entire countries—the Baltic states of Estonia, Latvia, and Lithuania. These countries on the Baltic Sea had been formed from Russian territory after her defeat in World War I and had been guaranteed their independence by Lenin. Now the Soviets took them back and made them Union Republics. Several countries, including the United States and Great Britain, are still demanding their return to independence and maintain diplomatic relations with their leaders in exile—little more than a gallant gesture.

On June 22, 1941, the Germans broke the Nazi-Soviet Pact and invaded the Soviet Union to start what the Soviets call "The Great Patriotic War." In short order the Nazis occupied the Baltic region and the industrial Donets Basin, were beseiging Leningrad and threatening Moscow. The Nazis turned the Baltic states and the Belorussian Republic into "Ostland," a commissariat of the Third Reich. Some of the people of the Baltic states welcomed the Germans as liberators, a natural reaction of a people conquered only shortly before, and collaborated with the Nazis. Noncollaborators were sent off to

Germany as slave laborers or were executed by the SS, who committed numerous atrocities. Those Ostlanders who managed to escape the Nazis found themselves in new peril when the Soviets recaptured the area. Thousands of them were sent to Siberia or executed along with true collaborators. Executions of those accused of being Ostlander collaborators were still being carried out until at least 1980; an accused collaborator was extradited from the United States to the Soviet Union in 1987.

Soviet citizens of German descent were also sent to Siberia, either to camps or as "special settlers" under the supervision of one security organ or another. And the Volga German Autonomous Republic, formed after the October Revolution for Soviet citizens of German descent, was dissolved.

(It might be noted here that the United States sent its citizens and residents of Japanese extraction to internment camps after the bombing of Pearl Harbor. The unannounced attack, with its many casualties, the fear of invasion and possible betrayal from within, and reports of Japanese atrocities in prisoner-of-war camps and of death marches, led to this decision. Today, there are some who equate the Soviet corrective labor camps and the Nazi concentration camps with the American detention camps for the Japanese in the United States. Nothing could be further from the truth. While the American camps were far from luxurious, and these innocent Japanese suffered humiliation and economic and emotional distress from their detention, no one was killed, no one was shot or gassed or incinerated or tortured or beaten or starved or experimented upon medically. Children were not torn away from parents, women were not forced into prostitution, people were not bestialized as in Soviet and Nazi camps.)

By 1942–1943, reports of forced labor camps in Siberia

began reaching the West from Poles being sent home by terms of the Soviet-Polish Treaty. Again, the reports were not believed. In 1944, the Vice President of the United States, Henry A. Wallace, and Owen Lattimore of the U.S. Office of War Information, made a celebrated three-day stopover in Siberia on their way to China, in part to see for themselves what the truth of the situation was. They were on the grounds of an actual corrective labor camp—completely changed for the visit. They did not learn until later of the prisoners who were hidden from them deep in the *taiga,* of barbed wire and watchtowers torn down and shopwindows specially stocked for the visit, of NKVD staff acting as farm workers—happy volunteers—and of many other deceptions played upon them. On their return to the United States the men gave interviews and wrote books denying the existence of labor camps and praising the spirit and energy of the country as superior not only to that of Imperial Russia but also to that of the United States. Mr. Wallace later apologized for being so gullible. But, in the meanwhile, Stalin's intent to deceive the West about the Soviet system had been successful. It took many years for well-meaning people who wanted to believe in what they felt were the good things of communism to accept the reality of Siberian prison camps.

In February, 1945, the heads of government of Great Britain and the United States—Winston Churchill and Franklin Delano Roosevelt—went to the Crimea for a meeting with Stalin. Known as the Yalta Conference, it was here that plans were made for the end of the war in Europe and affirming the division and occupation of Germany. Among the agreements that affected Siberia was one to return Soviet nationals from abroad. *Smersh,* the Russian abbreviation for "death to the spies," was not a James Bond fiction but the name of the security group created to arrest and exile or execute any suspects among those who had lived outside of Soviet influence during the war: Soviet refugees and deportees; the Soviet citizens of the Baltic republics, Belorussia, and other territory that had been occupied by the Germans; and even Soviet forces occupying conquered countries and returning prisoners of war. Stalin believed that true patriotic Soviet soldiers would not have allowed themselves to be taken prisoner. Until recently this concern with defilement by outside influences strongly affected the policies of the Soviet Union, revealing not only a paranoid fear of an enemy in every bush, but a deep insecurity, a belief that Soviet citizens will invariably prefer other places, other ways, when they find out about them.

There were several other Yalta agreements affecting Siberia, some not made public until 1947. They involved the disposition of the Japanese Empire at the end of the war. Japan was to be stripped of all the territory she had acquired as the result of her course of imperialist expansion. The Soviet Union was to get back her losses from the Russo-Japanese War of 1905—Port Arthur and the Trans-Siberian Railway right-of-way in Manchuria. She was also to receive the northern part of Korea—part of the Japanese Empire since 1910—and the Kurile Islands. All these concessions were contingent on a Soviet declaration of war on Japan within three months of the end of the war in Europe. The United States and the countries of the British Commonwealth had been fighting on the Pacific front for almost four years, and Roosevelt and Churchill felt they needed Stalin's troops to end the war. It turned out that they didn't.

The war in Europe ended on May 8, 1945, and exactly three months to the day, on August 8, and not one day sooner, Stalin kept to the letter of the bargain and declared war on

Stalin requested this U.S. Coast Guard cutter, the ultimate in icebreakers at the time, as part of Lend-Lease.

Japan. He kept to the letter, but not the spirit. He gave no help to the Allies. By then it was two days after the atomic bomb had been dropped on Hiroshima, and all the world was aware that it was only a matter of days before the war ended. Stalin's late and unnecessary entry into the war was almost a gesture of contempt. He would get all he had been promised at Yalta without expending any effort, without having to give anything. Actually, Stalin's declaration of war on Japan was just a matter of insurance. He had already sent in the Red Army to get all but one of the concessions he had been offered in that one-sided bargain at Yalta.

The Manchurian territory promised to Stalin at Yalta had seen a number of changes since the Russian leases had been turned over to Japan in 1905 by the Treaty of Portsmouth. That foothold in Manchuria had given Japan the opportunity to take the rest of that Chinese province in 1931–32 when she started her long Second War with China. Having gone that far, Japan went further. She added to Manchuria the neighboring province of Jehol, creating Manchukuo, a puppet state, supposedly independent but actually controlled by Japan, with the former emperor of China at its head. The Yalta agreement had ignored the fact that Port Arthur and the old Trans-Siberian right-of-way had only been leased to Imperial Russia. They belonged to China, and China expected them back when Japan was stripped of her empire. Stalin was not one to wait patiently for territorial rights to be sorted out. He insured himself of his rights to the old leases by making his move before rights became an issue. Before he started his war with Japan, before the Yalta agreements could be made public, Stalin sent in his Red Army, assisted by the Mongolian Army, and took all of Manchukuo, not just the part promised at Yalta. After the war, the Chinese—the Nationalist Chinese then in power—protested the Soviet takeover. The Soviets returned the two provinces of Manchuria and Jehol in May, 1946, but not before helping the enemies of the Nationalists, the Communist Chinese, to secure the area for themselves.

At the same time as Soviet troops took Manchukuo, they also invaded Korea. Korea was promised her independence at the Cairo Conference of 1943 between the United States, Great Britain, and China. Yalta's proposed division of Korea was contrary to that agreement and again was not a proper gift. And again Soviet conquest, without a declaration of war and before World War II ended, took care of the entire matter.

After the war, Korea was simply divided into two occupation zones at the 38th parallel—latitude 38° N.—so that the Soviets could stay in the north. As relationships between the United States and the USSR worsened in what is called the "cold war," a United Nations trusteeship took Korea over. Two separate Korean governments were formed, North and South. But in June, 1950, the North Koreans launched a surprise invasion of South Korea. United Nations troops, including many thousands of Americans, were sent in to help South Korea, fighting Soviet-trained and -equipped North Koreans, and later Chinese, in the devastating Korean War, the stage having been set at Yalta.

The one Yalta offering that the Soviets did not take before they entered the war on Japan was the Kurile Islands. They waited for this until after the official surrender of the Japanese on September 2, 1945. Again, the Kuriles should not have been bartered at Yalta; they had not been part of any Japanese Imperialist expansion. The Kuriles and Sakhalin had been settled and administered by Japan and Russia jointly from the 1700s until 1875, when the two countries agreed on a split: Russia to take Sakhalin, Japan the Kuriles, which she named Chishima-Retto. Now the Soviet Union had both.

The Kuriles consist of about thirty larger islands and many tiny ones, some so small they don't make it onto a map. They are strung like links in a chain from Japan's northernmost border at Hokkaido to the southern tip of the Soviet Union's Kamchatka Peninsula in Siberia. Today they are highly explosive, and not only because of their thirty-eight active volcanoes and recurrent earthquakes.

Japan wants the islands, now part of Sakhalin Oblast in Siberia. She is making their return a preliminary to any commercial or political negotiations between the two countries, including a treaty of peace, so there is a lot of diplomatic maneuvering going on.

On Iturup Island (the Japanese call it Etorofu) in the Kurile chain, the Soviets have stationed some 10,000 troops, 40 MiG-23 jets, and an unknown number of nuclear-capable missiles. Iturup/Etorofu is only ten miles from Hokkaido, too close for Japanese comfort. Several violations of Japanese airspace have already occurred, so far without fatal consequence, unlike the Korean Airlines flight 007 that flew into Soviet airspace over the Kuriles and Sakhalin in 1985 and was shot down with a loss of several hundred innocent passengers.

Japan is an antinuclear country and understandably sensitive to the nuclear weapons positioned just a few miles away. She also objects to the special mapping techniques being developed by the Siberian branch of the Academy of Sciences, intended to pinpoint good places for settlement on the Kuriles. Settlement will make any return of the islands to Japan even less likely.

The Soviets are eager to trade their vast resources of Siberian oil and natural gas for Japan's highly desirable technology, but it is unlikely that they would give back the Kuriles. The Soviets need the island chain, because it lies across the neck that separates the Sea of Okhotsk from the Pacific Ocean. An unfriendly power holding the chain can strangle the Soviets' access to the Pacific.

The Soviet Union is very defense-conscious, and very defensive about the rest of the world seeing her as backward—a kind of national paranoia or persecution complex. Actually, the Soviets, and the Russian Empire before them, have been very canny in their dealings with the rest of the world. They have won at the treaty tables even when they have lost wars, and they have gained far more than any of their allies from victory. Their accomplishments in space and in the arts of Imperial Russia have brought them worldwide admiration. But their social and individual gains, and even their huge industries, have not all kept pace. And the development of Siberia, although widely publicized, has fallen far short of its potential. Every leader of the Soviet Union has promised great things for Siberia—one day. Perhaps the new Soviet leader, Mikhail Gorbachev, and his policy of "glasnost" or openness, responsiveness, will make today that day. Or tomorrow.

10

Behind the Iron/Ice Curtain

SOON AFTER World War II ended, 2,000 scientists met to discuss plans for the economic development of Siberia. Not long afterward, there was still another conference on the subject, this time with 4,000 scientists. Whatever their ideas, it lay with the political leaders of the country to do as they wished with Siberia. Lenin had stressed the importance of developing Siberia, of creating industries close to the great Siberian sources of raw materials. Stalin's Five-Year Plans began the development of the Kuzbas, the Kuznetsk Basin at the foot of the Altai Mountains in Western Siberia. The Kuzbas holds one of the world's richest coal and iron deposits, and gives the Soviet Union a metalurgical-defense area second only to the great Don Basin-Leningrad or Donbas area. But it was Nikita Khrushchev who really tackled the development of Siberia.

Nikita Khrushchev was made First Secretary of the Communist Party in 1953 after Stalin's death. (He was to become head of the Soviet Union in 1957–58.) Stalin's final years had been marked by increasing mental instability that caused worsening conditions in Siberian prison camps and a virtual repeat of the Great Purge. His growing anti-Semitism and demand for Russianization had threatened all minorities. When Stalin died, his right-hand man, the dreaded head of security, Lavrentiy Beria, expected to succeed to his place. Fortunately for the people, and particularly the prisoners of Siberia, a more moderate coalition of leaders was able to defeat Beria and take over the reins of government. Beria was shot as an "imperialist agent," whatever that is supposed to mean, but his death probably saved millions of lives.

The new coalition government was anxious to de-Stalinize the country. The security organs were given a less dominant role in Soviet life and politics. Prisoners in a few Siberian camps even dared to strike in protest over conditions and lived to tell of it. Jehovah's Witnesses, a religious sect new to the Soviet Union and particularly persecuted for their defiance of all authority but the heavenly, played a prominent role in the strikes. De-Stalinization progressed rapidly after a secret report given by First Secretary Khrushchev to the Communist party's Twentieth Congress in 1956. The report revealed Stalin's evils and condemned his abuses. Minority nationalities were "rehabilitated"—returned to their former status and homes—except for those of German descent, who only received recognition as an ethnic minority. A number of legal reforms were made, arbitrary arrests were curtailed, and many prisoners released from Siberian imprisonment. The camps were supposed to have been closed in the 1960s, but later reports showed some were still in use in the 1970s. Psychiatric hospitals, to attempt to change behavior, and house arrest and exile to carefully guarded closed regions are also replacing Siberian

Nikita Khrushchev

exile for politicals, or dissidents, as they are now called. Reports coming from the Soviet Union say that some camps still exist in the far northeast of Siberia. One can only hope they are more humane than the camps of Stalin's time.

Agriculture had been exploited and destroyed by Stalin, but Khrushchev, from a peasant family, understood the importance of agriculture to the Soviet Union and to Siberia in particular. Siberian diets, like those of other peoples in Arctic and subarctic lands, are heavily dependent on meat and fish. Reindeer herds supply a lot of that meat, the rivers a lot of fish. But about 98 percent of the population of Siberia is Russian and Ukrainian, and they also eat a great deal of bread, and bread requires the growing of grain. So does the keeping of livestock. Khrushchev organized the Virgin Land Campaign in 1953 to put unused land and reclaimed wasteland in Siberia into grain production. Young couples in particular were recruited for the project, possibly against their will as expert observers of Soviet affairs have said, although they were depicted in movies and newspapers and magazines as stalwart, happy builders of a new world. Still, in a few years they had put almost 88,000,000 acres under cultivation.

Agriculture, or the lack of it, is still a major problem in the development of Siberia. Growing things is difficult where so much of the land is permafrost—perpetually frozen soil. Much effort is going into research on special techniques like greenhousing and hydroponics, growing plants in water. In the south where there is no permafrost, the land is either cultivated or arid. There is a long-range plan to turn Siberia's great north-flowing rivers around to help the farmers in arid lands in the south. Instead of emptying into the Arctic Ocean, the rivers would be routed into small south-flowing rivers, making them large enough to be dammed for irrigation projects.

Siberia is blessed with rivers—anywhere from 53,000 to 155,000, depending on how broad your definition of a river is. A swiftly flowing river or one that falls from one height to another can be used to turn turbines that create electric power. So Khrushchev added electrification to his drive to develop Siberia. A famous and oft-quoted statement of Lenin's, "Communism is Soviet power plus electrification of the whole country," has been taken very seriously in Siberia. Communism there must be flourishing, because electrification is running rampant. As yet, all that power cannot be relayed the distances necessary to service the rest of the Soviet Union, but solutions to that problem are in the offing.

The huge Bratsk hydroelectric plant on the Angara River

The hydroelectric plant at Zeya in the Far Eastern region of Siberia.

was started in 1954. To dam the river for the plant, trucks lined up day and night, pouring rocks into the swift waters without a stop. Stopping would let the powerful river tear it all down. This was a new concept in building dams, which are usually poured-concrete. The Bratsk dam is one of the largest in the world, its reservoir 550 kilometers long. The plant also has the distinction of having an important poem written in its honor, "The Bratsk Hydroelectric Station," by Yevgeny Yevtushenko, one of the world's most famous living poets. This may seem to you a strange subject for poetry, but in the Soviet Union this is the way it is. Hydroelectricity in Siberia is the theme or background of many novels and plays. This does show how proud the Soviet people are of their achievements in this area. On the other hand, it also shows the severe limitations put on Soviet artists. They are allowed to portray only certain subjects in particular forms. Until recently, rock music was taboo, and hard rock still is. The government sees it as their business to control freedom of artistic expression to discourage dissent and encourage support for their projects, but the Soviets also have rigid ideas of what is "proper." In a 1986 interview in *The New York Times*, the head of Siberia's Irkutsk Oblast, which is bigger than Texas, said, "We have 35 members of the writers' union in Irkutsk Oblast, 65 people in the artists' union, and 205 actors. There are huge construction projects at the Bratsk and Ust-Ilimsk hydro stations and there is the Bratsk forest-industry complex, so there is plenty of material for our artists to depict." Concrete and wood—sturdy materials. None of that mushy stuff for stalwart Soviet citizens!

Yet Siberians call the Angara River "the Beauty Queen" and tell a lovely story about her. It seems that Angara is one of 336 beautiful daughters of the great Lake Baikal. Father Baikal waited every night for his many daughters to make their way across the mountains to him before he would sleep. But one day Angara fell in love with the mighty warrior river, Yenisei, and yearned to join him. She pined away, until one night as Father Baikal was sleeping very soundly, Angara ran off and flung herself toward Yenisei. Father Baikal awoke and was very angry at his disobedient daughter. He tossed a huge rock at Angara to stop her, but she was too quick for him. He could not keep her from her rendezvous with Yenisei. And thus the Angara is the only river to flow out of Lake Baikal, although 335 rivers empty into this deepest lake in the world.

It is Angara's very speed in escaping Father Baikal that makes her so suitable for the Bratsk and Ust-Ilimsk hydro stations, and fourteen more planned for her. Her lover, the great Yenisei, has a hydro station of his own at Krasnoyarsk with the largest capacity in the world. Six more stations are planned for the Yenisei. A project on the Lena River will be two or three times larger even than the one at Krasnoyarsk, and still more rivers will see numerous hydro stations. There's a lot of energy in Siberia but still not enough energy-consuming industries. Industrial development of Siberia is highly publicized, but it is moving slowly.

Developing Siberia is difficult and expensive. Half of Siberia is swamp, at least in the warmer months when the surface ice melts. The permafrost is unable to absorb the moisture, which just stays on top of the ground and spreads. And building on permafrost is a gigantic problem. The heat from any structure—be it buildings or bridges, roads or railway tracks—melts the top of the permafrost up to depths of six feet, and the structure promptly sinks, sways, bends, and cracks. Techniques are being developed to cope with permafrost, like putting buildings on special stilts. Permafrost may

Housing at a new industrial complex in Siberia.

even prove useful, since the cementlike ground can be tunneled and used as oil pipelines, and there's a lot of valuable oil and natural gas in the permafrost zone.

At each planned site for a hydroelectric station, or any other industrial complex, a town is built with schools, a recreation center, a hospital and baby clinics. This is Soviet law, and therefore the towns are all the same, whether 200 or 2,000 workers are to use them, whether they duplicate a town five minutes away or are the only settled area within a thousand miles. This uniformity is meant to be good, to treat everyone the same way, but it also results in boring, ingrown cities where everybody works and plays at the same things.

Siberia suffers from a lack of amenities. Indoor bathrooms and running water are expensive in the frozen north. Drinking water is delivered by small trucks that decant it into the customers' containers. In more remote areas it comes from

slabs of ice that are brought indoors and melted, and milk is
also sold in frozen blocks that have a wooden handle inserted
in them for easier carrying—like a giant popsicle. It is hard to
overlook the cold. Yet Verkhoyansk in northeast Siberia is a
bustling city. Verkhoyansk is the "Cold Pole" of the northern
hemisphere, with winter temperatures going down to almost
$-90°$ F. Perhaps bustling isn't quite the right word. In that
kind of cold, or even less, you can't move quickly. A sudden
intake of air into the throat can do major damage to the
respiratory system. You can hear your breath turning to ice,
and any uncovered skin is apt to get frostbite in minutes.
People watch one another in the bus lines or wherever for
signs of frostbite, but healing patches of skin on many a face
show it can be an unsuccessful battle. This kind of thing does
not appeal to everyone, and often means the loss of experienced
workers once their contracts are up.

Many incentives are given workers to sign contracts to
work in Siberia, and more to stay on. There may be extended
leaves, free food, free school uniforms, higher than ordinary
wages, and promises of quick advancement. For lack of more
experienced help, those barely out of school may be made
chiefs of divisions such as engineering and public transportation
in remote cities. There are many young people in Siberia.
Young people must perform so-called voluntary service or
enlist in the military for a period of two years. (Naval service
and work periods for those who receive school deferments are
longer.) Young people who have come to the West from the
Soviet Union say that it's mostly the unlucky ones who get to
go to Siberia, the ones who do not have enough "blat"—cannot
pull enough strings—to get out of it.

Transportation in Siberia is also still a problem. There is
limited plane service, reported as disorganized and somewhat

like freight cars. The Trans-Siberian Railway has had branches added, and the tracks for the Baikal-Amur Mainline were linked up in 1986. Two thousand miles long, the new line is intended to help develop Eastern Siberia's resources of timber and minerals like copper and asbestos. The tracks cross 22 mountain ranges, 17 major rivers, and thousands of minor ones. Its construction took ten years, and many years of work lie ahead in completing tunnels, stations, and settlements along the right-of-way. Again, settlement will be a problem—the terrain is harsh. But the tracks run 100 to 300 miles north of the Trans-Siberian tracks, farther from the uneasy Chinese border.

Transportation in the north, and between north and south, is more limited. There is only one major highway running north and south. East of Chita in Far Eastern Siberia, the road runs between the Trans-Siberian Railway and Yakutsk, some 700 miles to the north. In the north the frozen rivers are the roads, and when they are not frozen boat traffic is heavy. The Northern Sea Route feeds the rivers with goods. The Route is actually the long-sought Northeast Passage, one of the fabled water routes to the Orient from western Europe. The Passage, from the Barents Sea on the west to the Bering Sea on the east, was crossed for the first time in 1878–1879 by the Swedish explorer, N.A.E. Nordenskjöld. That was a good while before another Swede, Roald Amundsen, made the first crossing of the even more sought-after Northwest Passage. The Northwest Passage is not commercially practical, but the Northeast Passage has proven to be economically important. Its commercial value was first proven in 1913 when the great explorer and human-itarian, Fridtjof Nansen, accompanied a Russian group on a voyage from the Barents Sea to the Kara Sea and up the Yenisei River, bringing goods into the very center of Siberia, helping develop the area. However, the entire passage from the Barents

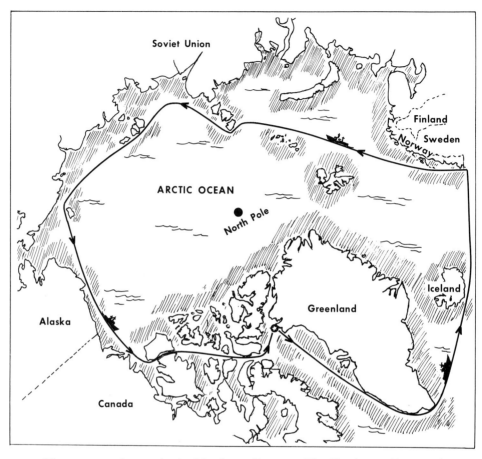

The route at the top is the Northeast Passage. The Northwest Passage is shown at the bottom, from Alaska to Greenland.

to Bering seas could not be made in one year. Winter ice closed the Passage in September or October and did not recede until June. Until a ship could cross without waiting over the winter, the Route was little more than a milestone discovery. Then in 1932, an Arctic explorer and mathematician named Otto Yulyevich Shmidt made the voyage across within one season, and northern Siberia was opened to development.

Shmidt is little known in the West, but was an important explorer of the Arctic. He set up the first floating ice station at the North Pole, and headed an expedition famous in Arctic annals in 1933. His ship, the *Chelyuskin,* was trapped in ice and had to be abandoned. The 111 members of the expedition had to live on the ice until they were rescued by daring feats of aviation that captured the attention and admiration of the world. The now-famous title "Hero of the Soviet Union" was awarded for the first time to honor the pilots who performed the rescues. Shmidt was made director of the Northern Sea Route in 1932 and as such administered the economic development of northern Siberia during the '30s until he lost his job—but not his life—during the Great Purge.

Today's ocean-going ships crossing the Route are too big for Siberia's rivers, so trans-shipment of goods into smaller ships and barges is necessary. But the Route is still economically important, and politically important as well. In World War II, the Route was kept open by American icebreakers on lend-lease. The money was never paid by the Soviets for either icebreakers or any other "leased" equipment or war loans, amounting to over a billion dollars. A token gesture toward returning the loaned ships was made, but most were in such bad condition they had to be scrapped. A United States Coast Guard cutter traveled through part of the Route in the '60s, insisting, as did other countries, that it was in international waters and thus open to all. The ship was called back when the U.S. State Department changed its mind about challenging the Soviets. The United States is still insistent on her right to travel the Route and the Soviets are equally insistent about it being territorial waters, not open to other countries without her permission. The Soviets have come up with what seems to be an answer: a toll. This allows both territoriality and international shipping—and adds a lot of money to the state treasury.

The Soviet Union today has an outstanding fleet of ice-breakers that keep the Northern Sea Route open from June to September; nothing can keep it open in the winter. Even in summer the ice can be formidable. In 1983, several ships were caught by the ice and one was crushed before the icebreakers could rescue them. In 1985, the icebreakers saved thousands of white beluga whales, breaking a channel through the ice that was stranding them.

In the far north, travel by sled with dogs or reindeer is not uncommon, although snowmobiles are fast gaining favor. In the south near Mongolia and the Old Silk Road, you can still see an occasional camel caravan. Siberia is nothing if not diverse.

The peoples of Siberia are equally diverse. They may be descendants of the "old settlers," *promyshlenniki* or prisoners or government bureaucrats or soldiers and Cossacks of the seventeenth and eighteenth centuries. Or they may be called "new" if their ancestors arrived in the nineteenth century. About 98 percent are Russian-Ukrainian. Another 1 percent are minority Poles, Germans, Jews (who are considered an ethnic, not a religious minority), Chinese, and others. There are about 150 different minorities in Siberia, including the "small peoples"—natives who are small in numbers, not in size—who make up the remaining 1 percent of the population.

Minorities may be organized into particular Autonomous Republics, Autonomous Oblasts, or National Okrugs, depending on their numbers. This does not mean that no one else can live there. They are not reservations, and Russians predominate everywhere. These administrative divisions were, however, based on a good idea: to keep minorities from being swamped by the numerically overwhelming Great Russian population. Then Stalin demanded conformity to the majority—Great Russian—ways and the original purpose was lost. Today, minority customs are somewhat encouraged, or at least not altogether discouraged, although autonomy does not exist despite the use of the word. The administrative divisions do offer some feeling of place, but they are primarily units of government. They must echo the dictates of the Communist Party Central Committee. They may have voting rights, but that vote is entirely meaningless and must follow the Party line.

Siberia has three Autonomous Republics (ASSRs) for larger minorities: the Yakut ASSR or Yakutia for the Turkic-speaking Yakuts, the Buryat ASSR for the Buryat Mongols, and the Tuva ASSR for the Tuvinians. Interestingly, in Yakutia the Russians seem to have assimilated with the Yakuts rather than the usual other way around, and many consider themselves Yakuts and speak the language.

The Tuvinians were conquered by the Mongol hordes, made subject to the Chinese Empire until 1912, and in 1917 given independence by the Bolsheviks. They had their own state, the Tuvinian People's Republic or Tannu-Tuva, but lost their independence in 1944 and became part of the Soviet Union. They were absorbed so quietly and with so little interest to the world that many mapmakers didn't find out about it for years.

Other minority groups in Siberia have enough members to qualify for Autonomous Oblasts or the smaller National Okrugs. The Mountainous-Altay have an Autonomous Oblast. They are not a single people historically, but were collected up and made into one by the Soviet Union in the 1920s because their various tribes spoke the same language and had roughly the same hunting culture. This same kind of collecting together of minorities applies to the Ostyaks (formerly Khanty) and the Voguls (formerly Mansi) who were gathered up in the Khanty-

Some natives of Siberia in the early twentieth century in traditional dress:
Samoyeds (top), a Yakut (right), and a group of Kirgiz.

Mansi National Okrug. The Tungus, those people involved in the mysterious great explosion of meteorite or spaceship, were renamed Evenki and given the Evenki National Okrug.

There are many other small peoples like the Samoyeds, the Chukchi, the Kamchatkans, and the almost extinct Golds of more ancient descent than even the Chinese and Koreans. But they are too few in number for even an Okrug.

Although they are not considered one of the "small peoples," the Jews are another minority with their own Oblast in Far Eastern Siberia. The Jewish Autonomous Oblast was carved out of Khabarovsk Kray on a bend of the Amur River in 1934. Its creation by the new Soviet government continued the old Russian characterization of Jews as an ethnic group, separate from Russians. The Jews are not one ethnic group and the idea of trying to function together in what they saw as a ghetto in dreaded Siberia was rejected by many Jews who preferred assimilation with their fellow Russians. The Jews have never been assimilated, however, and their passports still identify them as Jewish rather than Russian. Three million Soviet Jews could have been saved from death at the hands of the Nazis if this had not been so. Today, the Jewish Autonomous Oblast has a population that is only 6 percent Jewish. It is also a region designated as "closed," possibly because of its gold mines and scientific research.

A city or region may be closed because of its industries—like Gorky, the Soviet Detroit—or the research or mining going on. That not only keeps foreigners out but citizens in; special regulations apply to those who want to travel to somewhere else in the country or to change jobs. Traveling or changing jobs is not easy in the Soviet Union under any circumstances. Most persons over the age of sixteen must carry at all times an internal passport that records personal statistics, ethnicity, marital status, and all changes of residence and employment, including imprisonment. Details from the internal passport are entered in house books, kept in all multiple dwellings and hotels. Staying with friends in an apartment for a day or two calls for entry in the house book. Internal passports must be surrendered when people take jobs in closed regions and certain industries—mining, defense, transportation, banking. This makes it easy to control those in sensitive occupations; without their internal passports they can't move at all. Many members of the peasant class may not be issued internal passports in the first place. They are, therefore, severely restricted in their choices of work and in their movements. This binds them to the land like the serfs of yesterday, although they are employed by the government instead of owned.

The peasant class and the working class are supposedly the only classes in the Soviet Union. Another group, the educated intelligentsia, are not considered a class but as floaters moving among the two classes to serve them. Actually, there are other classes. A high party official may be a member of the working class, but certainly not in a class financially or socially with the women workers who sweep the streets. Whatever their class, people are regarded as tools for the good of the state, who is everyone's employer and guardian. The Communist party, the state, can do no wrong. When something does go wrong, it is the fault of the tools. The newspapers are full of letters from people doing penance by criticizing themselves for failing the party in one way or another. The newspapers, controlled by the government, act as watchdog agencies for the state, scolding or praising the workers and calling for their better performance or conduct. The Moscow press in particular has considerable power in monitoring local governments and issues in Siberia.

Issues are usually a matter of norms, of productivity. Issues like environmental protection that are so strong in the West are not a concern of the Soviet people in general. Most are not even aware of environmental problems. Only scientists and writers are allowed to address these concerns in careful letters to the newspapers or at professional meetings. Today, for instance, a few of them are protesting the plan to turn Siberia's rivers from their exits into the Arctic Ocean, pointing out that the changes in the ocean would harm the entire Arctic. The people do not protest their government's nuclear tests. They feel their government is interested only in peace and nuclear armaments are necessary for peace. Antinuclear protests in the United States and other countries only prove that those countries are interested in war. The press is quick to point the finger of blame at other countries. Currently they are fussing about acid rain—the fallout of chemicals that have been carried on air currents to drop in rain and snow far from where they originated in the smoke of factory chimneys, polluting water supplies. But it took the Soviets a while to understand why other countries should worry about the fallout carried by air currents from the explosion and fire at their nuclear plant in Chernobyl. Seemingly the Soviets consider the currents are moving one way only—toward them.

The government entrusts the safety of the environment to the ministries in charge of industrial and agricultural production. As yet there is no independent organization like the Environmental Protection Agency in the United States to monitor the environment. Since Soviet ministries must see to it that production quotas are met and costs kept down, expensive safeguards that may be time-consuming to install do not have a high priority. Much is made of the fact that one paper pulp plant near Lake Baikal installed waste-treatment equipment to avoid polluting the water.

Some effort is going into restoring strip-mining areas in the Arctic, and there may now be laws regulating that environmentally destructive method of mining. And there are a few nature preserves or *zapovedniki*. These are areas reserved for research and educational purposes, supposedly forever. Actually, they can be reduced in size or abolished, or used for growing hay and pasturing.

The Soviet government is becoming more active in environmental protection in view of world concern. Moscow says it has spent billions of dollars in the last decade for environmental controls, but what these are is largely unknown. They are leading the international program to protect the polar bear, and have a joint agreement with the United States, renewed in 1985, to study 38 environmental problems, including the effects of acid rain on forests, the pollution of underground water, and toxic waste treatment.

It is comforting to know that there are some areas of cooperation between the Soviet Union and the United States, who have been at odds over one thing or another since the end of World War II. The "cold war" between the two powers has more than once threatened to become a shooting war, and high in the Arctic both countries stand at the ready with tracking, warning, defense, and counterattack systems aiming at one another across the top of the world. A great deal of money is being poured into Siberia for the development of these systems and also to make this Asian section of the country more strategically important.

From the time of Peter the Great, Russia fought to become a leading power in Europe. The Soviets have accomplished this, and recognize that Siberia can make them a dominant power in Asia as well. They are pouring vast sums into developing Siberia and increasing their Pacific military presence. Some Soviet officials feel that too much money is going into Siberia. Too much spent on dams, and not enough on damsels—and men—is the complaint. They want the country to be powerful, but they want the people to live better, too. The average Soviet citizen still has to stand on long lines to buy things like toilet paper, soap, clothes. Two or three families may share one apartment, and indoor toilets and privacy are luxuries many people do not have. While the standard of living is better than it once was, it is still not up to the standards of many other countries.

The Soviets are seeking to increase their income by encouraging tourism, a very lucrative business. Along with Moscow and Leningrad, the great tourist attraction is Siberia and particularly the fabled Trans-Siberian Railway. Many people are unaware that tourists can visit Siberia. Siberia is so remote, so unknown, its history as a prison so chilling, that few people realize it is also a place of vast natural splendors and large, sophisticated cities. Anyone with enough money and the proper documents can travel through Siberia—or at least some of it. There are many restrictions and closed regions in the north and Far East, including the city of Vladivostok and the Jewish Autonomous Oblast.

Because of this close control, travelers do not see the Siberian wilderness or meet many Siberians, especially not natives. The cities and the hydroelectric stations are their lot, not the fabled wolves of Siberia (some with bright red hair) or the saber-toothed tigers or snow leopards or even the world-famous Russian sables, minks, and ermines. But Lake Baikal is a mandatory stop for tourists in Siberia. In winter the beloved

Russian bears may be seen as they amble onto the lake to catch fish through the holes in the ice obligingly made for them by the Buryat natives. The tourist may also see the yellow fog that some say comes from the trapped breaths of thousands of people and animals in the frozen atmosphere. There are also seals in Lake Baikal, the only fresh-water seals in the world, and many fish found in no other waters, like the oumoul or Baikal salmon and the strange transparent fish that dissolves in sunlight, leaving behind a valuable oil. With good planning, the visitor may see the tangled *taiga* by the light of a full moon, or the sun rise a glorious green over thousands of miles of uninhabited land, or the huge scar made by that fearful explosion in 1908.

And perhaps the traveler will feel in the cold winds something of the sorrow of the millions of men, women, and children who died in the prison camps of Siberia and be glad to think of this Siberia as winding its way into history to become the Siberia that may finally fulfill the promise of its great natural resources.

Index

Academy of Sciences, 12–13, 118
Acid rain, 138, 139
Agriculture, 122, 123
Alaska, 39, 42, 43, 44
Albert, Prince (England), 65
Aleutian Islands, 42, 43, 44
Alexander II, Czar, 43, 59, 90
Alexander III, Czar, 59
Alexandra, Czarina, 63, 65, 70
Alexei, Czarevitch, 65, 70
Alphabet, Russian, 9
Amundsen, Roald, 129
Amur River, 28, 36, 48–53
Angara River, 28, 123, 125–126
Anti-Semitism, 90, 121
Artels, 66, 87–88
Astrakhan, 23, 24
Atomic bomb, 115
Attila the Hun, 22

Baikal, Lake, 22, 28, 125–126, 140, 141

Baranov, Alexander, 42, 43
Baranov Island, 42
Belorussia, 3, 114
Beria, Lavrentiy, 104, 121
Bering, Vitus, 38–39, 42
Bering Sea, 39
Bering Strait, 39
Black Sea, 45
Blagoveschchensk, 50, 53
"Bloody Sunday," 59
Bolsheviks, 67, 69, 70, 73–74, 75, 98–99, 133
Bonner, Yelana, 8
Boxer Rebellion, 50, 53
Bratsk hydroelectric plant, 123, 125
Brest-Litovsk Treaty, 102

Cabot, Sebastian, 43
Cairo Conference (1943), 116
Calendar, Russian, 9
Cannibalism, 101
Cape Dezhnev, 38

Catherine the Great, 42
Central Asian Republics, 3, 6
Cheka, 69, 98
Chelyuskin (ship), 131
Chernobyl, 138
Chernozem, 7
Chishima-Retto. *See* Kurile Islands
Chita, 7, 79
Chukchi, 8, 136
Churchill, Winston, 113, 114
Class structure, 137
"Cold war," 139
Commander Islands, 39
Committee of State Security, 98
Committees of the Poor, 75
Communism, 68–69, 75, 100, 109,
    113, 123
Communist Party, 74, 75, 99, 102,
    133, 137
Concepción, Doña, 43–44
Cossacks, 24, 25, 26, 27, 28, 34, 45,
    50, 90
Crimea, 23, 24
Crimean War, 45, 48
Czechs, 70–71, 72

Dalstroy. *See* Gulag
Dates, Russian, 9
Day in the Life of Ivan Denisovich, A
    (Solzhenitsyn), 104
Decembrists, 78–79
Dekabrists. *See* Decembrists
De-Stalinization, 121
Dezhnev, Semeon Ivanovich, 38
Dictatorship of the Proletariat, 69
Dmitri, Czarevitch, 34
Donskoy, Dmitri, 23
Duma, 60, 65, 67

Eastern Slav Family, 19
Ekaterinburg, 9, 21
Electrification, 123
Engels, Friedrich, 68

Environmental problems, 138–139
Eskimos, 21
Estonia, 111
Etorofu. *See* Iturup Island
Evenki, 8, 136. *See also* Tungus
Explosion, Tunguska, 11–17

Feodor, Czar, 34
Five Year Plans, 106, 120
Furs, 22, 24, 26, 42

Gagarin, Prince, 38
Genghis Khan, 22
Godunov, Boris, 34
    map drawn under direction of,
    32–33
Golden Horde, 22–23, 26, 27
Golds, 136
Gorbachev, Mikhail, 119
Gorky, 136
Goths, 22
Great Northern Expedition, 39
Great Patriotic War, 111
Great Purge, 101–104, 121, 131
Guinsberg, Eugenia, 108
Gulag, 104, 105
Gulag Archipelago, 104

Hitler, Adolf, 99, 109, 111
Horde. *See* Golden Horde
Hydroelectricity, 123, 125–127

Indians, American, 21
Industrial Revolution, 59
Intelligentsia, 137
Irkutsk, 28, 83
Irtysh River, 26, 28
Islam, 23
Iturup Island, 118
Ivan, Czar, 37
Ivan III, Grand Prince of Muscovy,
    23
Ivan the Terrible, 23–24, 26, 31, 34,
    35

Janin, General, 72
Jehol, 116
Jehovah's Witnesses, 121
Jews, 90–91, 102, 109, 136

Kamchatka Peninsula, 45
Kamchatkans, 136
Kara Prison, 82, 91
Katorzhniki, 109
Kazakhstan, 3, 6
Kazan, 23, 24
Kazantsev, Alexsander, 15
Khabarov, Yerofei, 36
Khabarovsk, 36
Khrushchev, Nikita, 120–123
Kiev, 19
Kirov, Sergey Mironovich, 101
Kodiak Island, 42
Kolchak, Alexander Vasilyevich, 71, 72
Kolkhozes, 75, 99, 100
Komandorski Islands. *See* Commander Islands
Korea, 114, 116–117
Korean War, 117
Krasnoshchekov, Alexander, 72–73
Krasnoyarsk, 28, 66, 126
Krupskaya, Nadezhda, 8
Kuchum Khan, 24, 26
Kulaks, 75, 100
Kulik, Leonid, 13–15
Kurile Islands, 43, 44, 114, 117–118
Kuzbas, 120

Languages, 9
Laptev, Dmitri, 39
Laptev, Khariton, 39
Laptev Sea, 39
Lattimore, Owen, 113
Latvia, 111
Lena River, 28, 126
Lenin, Vladimir Ilich, 8, 67–69, 73,
74, 75, 76, 79, 98–101, 111, 120, 123
Leningrad, 8, 140
Liakhov (merchant), 42
Lithuania, 111

Magnitogorsk, 18
Mammoth, great woolly, 20, 21–22
Manchukuo, 116
Manchuria, 116
Maritime Territory, 50
Marx, Karl, 68
Mikhail, Czar, 35
Minority groups, 132–136
Mirs, 31
Mongols, 22, 23, 133
Monroe Doctrine, 44
Moscow, 6, 21, 34, 70, 140
Moscow Road (Track), 52, 80
Mountainous-Altay, 133
Muraviev, Nicholas Nicholayevitch, 48–51
Muraviev-Amurski, Count, 53
Muscovy, 21
Muscovy Company, 43
Muslims, 102

Names, Russian, 7–9
Nansen, Fridtjof, 129
Nazis, 111–112, 136
Nazi-Soviet Pact, 111
Nenets, 8
N.E.P. men, 75
Nerchinsk, Treaty of, 37, 48
New Archangel. *See* Sitka, Alaska
New Economic Policy, 75
New Siberian Islands, 39
Newspapers, 137
Nicholas I, Czar, 48, 77, 78
Nicholas II, Czar, 54, 56, 59, 60, 63, 64, 67, 70
Nordenskjöld, N.A.E., 129
Nordenskjöld Sea, 39

Northeast Passage, 129–130
Northern Sea Route, 129, 131–132
Northwest Passage, 129, 130
Novgorod, 21, 23
Novykh, Grigori Yefimovich. *See* Rasputin
Nuclear tests, 138

Ob River, 22
October Revolution (1917), 8, 9, 35, 67–70, 97, 98, 102, 103
Omsk, ostrag at, 29
Opium Wars, 49
Ostland, 111
Ostrogs, 28, 29
Ostyaks, 133

Patronymic names, 7
Pavlova, Anna, 7
Peasant Land Bank, 60
Peoples of Siberia, 132–133, 136–137
Permafrost, 126–127
Peter the Great, 8, 37–38, 39, 139
Place names, 8
Port Arthur, Manchuria, 56, 114, 116
Portsmouth, Treaty of, 56, 116
Poyarkov, Cossack, 28, 36
Pribilof, Gerasim, 42
Pribilof Islands, 42
Prisoners in Siberia, 77–97, 104–109
Promyshlenniki, 27–28, 29, 42, 45
Provisional Government, 67, 71
Purge. *See* Great Purge

Railroads. *See* Trans-Siberian Railway
Rasputin, 8, 65
Red Guards, 69, 71, 98
Rezanov, Nicolai Petrovich, 42–44
Rivers, 28, 53, 123, 129, 138. *See also* names of rivers
Romanov dynasty, 35

Roosevelt, Franklin D., 113, 114
Roosevelt, Theodore, 56
RSFSR. *See* Russian Soviet Federated Socialist Republic
Rus, 21
Russia. *See* Russian Soviet Federated Socialist Republic
Russia Company, 43
Russian America, 43–44
Russian American Company, 43
Russian Soviet Federated Socialist Republic, 3, 6
Russo-Japanese War, 54, 56, 114

Sakhalin Island, 44, 56, 73, 82, 92, 118
Sakharov, Andre, 8
Samizdat, 105
Samoyeds, 8, 136
Savirs, 22
Seals, fresh-water, 141
Serfs, 30–31, 34, 59
Serpantinka camp, 108
Seward, William H., 44
Shelikov, Gregori Ivanovich, 42
Shelikov Strait, 42
Shilka River, 37
Shmidt, Otto Yulyevich, 130–131
Shturmovoy mine, 108
Siberia
    autonomous republics of, 132, 133
    boundaries, 6–7, 18, 36, 37
    Central, 7, 11–17
    civil war in, 70
    early history of, 18–44
    Eastern, 7, 129
    exile system in, 34–35, 37, 76, 77–109
    expansion of, 36–44
    Far Eastern, 7, 45, 71, 73–74, 87, 129
    geography, 6
    location, 3, 6

northern, 130–131
origin of name, 22
peoples of, 132–133, 136–137
prisoners of, 77–109
size of, 6
Western, 7, 29, 71, 120
Sitka, Alaska, 42, 43, 44
Slavery, 30–31
Slavs, 19
Smersh, 113
Solzhenitsyn, Alexander, 104
Sophia Alexeyevna, 37
Soviet Union. *See* Union of Soviet
    Socialist Republics
Soviets of Workers' and Soldiers'
    Deputies, 67
Stalin, Josef, 8, 76, 99, 101–104, 106,
    111, 113, 114–116, 120–122, 132
Standard of living, 140
Steppes, 7, 29
Strait of Tatar, 48, 49
Strip mining, 139
Stroganovs, 24, 25, 26, 31
Surnames, Russian, 7
Sybir, 22

Taiga, 7, 11–12, 13, 26, 85, 141
Tamerlane, 22, 23, 72
Tannu-Tuva, 133
Tatar, Strait of, 48, 49
Tatars, 22, 23, 26
Taymyr, 8
"Time of Troubles," 34
Tobol River, 28
Tobolsk, 28
Tolstoy, Leo, 8
Tom River, 28
Tomsk, 28
Tourism, 140–141
Trans-Siberian Railway, 53–54, 56,
    60, 63, 70, 71, 72, 80, 84, 100,
    105, 114, 116, 129, 140
Transportation, 128–132

Troika (sleigh), 53
Troikas (tribunals), 99, 103
Trotsky, Leon, 70, 101–102
Tundra, 7
Tungus, 8, 12, 14, 136
Tungus River, 13
Tunguska explosion, 11–17
Turks, 24
Tuvinians, 133
Tver, 23

Uglich, 34
Union of Siberian Butter Artels, 66
Union of Soviet Socialist Republics
    administrative units, 3
    formation of, 73
    republics in, 3
Ural Mountains, 18–19, 21–22, 25,
    27
Ussuri River, 49, 51, 54

Verkhoyansk, 128
Victoria, Queen, 65
Vikings, 21, 23
Virgin Land Campaign, 123
Vladivostok, 49, 55, 63, 64, 71, 140
Volga German Autonomous
    Republic, 112
Voyevodsk Prison, 90

Wallace, Henry A., 113
Wilhelm, Kaiser, 65
Woravetlans, 8
World War I, 63–72
World War II, 110–117, 131

Yakutia, 133
Yakuts, 133
Yakutsk, 28, 88, 129
Yalta Conference, 113–116, 117
Yamal, 8
Yeneseisk, 28
Yenisei Man, 19, 21

Yenisei River, 28, 126, 129
Yermak, 25–26, 34
Yevtushenko, Yevgeny, 125
Yezhov, Nikolai, 101, 102, 104

Yezhovshchina. See Great Purge
Yugra, 22

Zeya, hydroelectric plant at, 124

MADELYN KLEIN ANDERSON is a graduate of Hunter College, New York University, and the Graduate School of Library and Information Science of Pratt Institute, New York. She is a former army officer and occupational therapist who moved into the publishing world and became a senior editor of children's books with a major publishing company before turning to writing full-time. She is the author of *Greenland: Island at the Top of the World,* among other titles for young readers.

Ms. Anderson has lived in many areas of the country, and has traveled extensively. She now makes her home in New York City.